The Man
I Called Father

The Man I Called Father

Surprised By Grace

❖

Paul Josephson

Litany Press
New York

© 2014 by Paul Josephson

All rights reserved

❖

To protect the privacy of living individuals, certain names in this account have been altered where it was felt appropriate to do so. The events described herein, on the other hand, are reported exactly as they happened, without embellishment of any kind.

❖

ISBN – 13: 978 1492896876
ISBN – 10: 149289687X

PUBLISHED BY LITANY PRESS
2014

Table of Contents

i
Introduction

1
The Fallow Beginnings

7
Seedings

92
A New Man

151
Liberation

185
The Man, My Father

Introduction

I LIVED FOR TWENTY YEARS with this man I call father. I lived with him as a son, a spiritual son, a relationship I hope to make meaningful to you before we are through. Let me say here, right off, that the man I write of devoted a fair amount of time and effort to bringing his spiritual charge, sometimes by cogent conversation and sometimes by the scruff of the neck, back to God. My problem wasn't that I didn't believe in God or gave no thought to Him; I simply could not believe that God could possibly love the likes of me. This man changed all that. When I became his spiritual son, I was already thirty-one and he was fifty-six.

He had been a professor of philosophy, with a reputation among his peers for being one of the most brilliant minds to be found anywhere. He was to become a *bona fide* Catholic mystic, but he started out quite otherwise, as an agnostic Jew who happened to think of himself as every bit as smart as Aristotle. But then, as he told it, one day he began to read St. Thomas's commentary on Aristotle, and he knew he had met up with a mind clearly superior to his own. Before long he followed that mind into the Church.

But by any measure this man was a behemoth among men, a man who simply towered over everyone

The Man I Called Father

else in sight, no matter where he was. He was not big physically but in every other respect he was larger than life, a most extraordinary man. In support, I cite some of the things you would have experienced had you known him: his astonishing intellect and wit; his lightening intuition (that made people think he could read your mind); his personality with its fascinating mixture of strength and tenderness; his shoot-from-the-hip way with humor; his patience and sometimes miraculous endurance with people that on other occasions could give way to profound yet unmistakably rational anger; his mysterious, soul-searching prowess at the piano; his profound spiritual poise and docility before God; and perhaps above everything, his peacefulness and his God-given way of instilling that peace in others. If this picture already eludes the mind, you must remember, that he was not a man who could be likened to other men.

And not surprisingly for so gifted a man, the whole story about him must acknowledge that there were hard edges as well. Not everyone esteemed him and eddies of controversy swirled about him all his adult life, and indeed continue to do so in some minds even today, more than thirty years after his death. Perhaps this was inevitable in a man who saw himself as God's instrument in the lives of those he came in real contact with.

I do not exaggerate when I call him peerless. He was indeed that, not only in the eyes of those around him, but in his own eyes as well. And that was the rub in any dealings with him. He insisted, as a matter of justice and truth, on being recognized for the intellectual and spiritual mentor that he was. It was as if he was congenitally unable to be anything less than master in

Introduction

relationships that mattered to him. Only God knows whether it was human pride or simple acknowledgment of the truth about himself that made him this way. But certainly this man saw himself as destined to serve God, first by interpreting God to others, much like a modern day St. Paul, and then by bringing those he instructed closer to God, which he did in many, many cases.

There was no evident trace of self-infatuation in him. He was not proud in the usual sense. He regarded all his endowments as coming from God, to be used as an instrument for God's purposes with souls. And just because he saw himself as God's instrument, as far as he was concerned, you could only be with him or against him. There was no middle ground. Either you acknowledged who he was, on his terms, or the relationship died. But here is the paradox, for once you acknowledged God's instrumentality in him for your life, he spent his life serving you, helping you, knocking you down sometimes but only to build you up, always working for your good and your salvation, indeed doing everything possible to give to you everything that he had to give, both materially and spiritually, no matter who you were. Many walked away after meeting him, smarting from the encounter; many saw him as insufferably overbearing, even boorish in his ways. But for those who got through the riptide beginnings and stayed the course, and there were many who did, the final impression was usually something rather different, more like the often-heard remark: *meeting this man was the best thing that ever happened in my life.*

He was known simply as "Doc" in those days, and I shall continue to call him by that name, in part out of respect for his own request for anonymity, conveyed to a priest before he died and duly reported to me. The account I give of him here deals principally with his relationship to me and my little family in the early stages of that relationship; it does not explain how he got to be the sort of person he was, how over a period of years he was changed from a brilliant philosophy professor to a profound, spiritual father, affecting the lives of many from all walks of life. The changes that took place in him are something between God and him, wrought in secret, and though I witnessed some portions of it, if I were to try and write of it I confess I would not know what I was talking about.

As I said at the start of this account, I (and I should add, a number of others) lived with this man for twenty years. What I describe here then is but the beginnings, the headwaters of a lengthy and at times arduous journey toward God. Perhaps someday a fuller story too can be told, but maybe it need not be, for as T. S. Eliot wrote in one of his last poems, our end is in our beginning. Hopefully, from the beginnings that are recounted here, one gets an idea of what that entire journey of the spirit must have been like.

Chapter One

The Fallow Beginnings

At the time I first heard of Doc, he was living in Mexico, engaged as a spiritual director to several convents of contemplative women religious. How a displaced New York Jew happened to be doing such a thing is interesting in its own right, and I try to account for it in the final chapter. But before that, I want to explain how I happened to get mixed up with this man, and what happened to me after I did. It all got started because of a young poet friend of mine.

Once every so often, Doc would receive a visit in Mexico from a young poet who had been one of his philosophy students at Xavier University in Cincinnati, and who now lived in New York's Greenwich Village. This young man, Howard Hart, in his early thirties, was an interesting combination of things: a more or less devout, if highly unconventional, Catholic; an exceptionally gifted poet; a pretty good jazz drummer; an inveterate bohemian who successfully avoided any hint of gainful employment all his life (thanks to his well-off businessman father who had left him with the necessary means); a good friend of Jack Kerouac and others of the so-called "beat generation"; and in general, a rather nervous individual who every so often went to Mexico to be with Doc as a way of quieting down and filling up his spiritual tank. And last but not least, Howie was my good friend, and the one who was to become my Godfather when one day I would enter the Church.

I used to wonder where he went those times he disappeared from the Village without explanation, especially when he would return in such a peaceful state of mind, his normally half-tortured face relaxed and actually glowing. Then one day he told me about his spiritual director and I said to him that if this man ever came to New York, I'd like to meet him. Which is exactly what happened.

The person whom Doc would meet in New York City, and not long thereafter adopt as his spiritual son, was born in that city in 1929. He would just turn 31 at the time of this encounter, in Greenwich Village in the Spring of 1960. His parents had been simple immigrants; his mother, the daughter of a Norwegian sea captain of a world-traveling sailing vessel, arrived here when she was but two years old, his father when he was twelve. His father, a self-educated man, overcame many hardships in his early life eventually to become president of a mid-size bank in Manhattan, and was thus able to raise and educate his four children in the kind of ease and comfort he himself had never known as a youth.

His parents were devout Lutherans and when their second son was ready for college at the callow age of 16, it was agreed that he should go to a Lutheran college in Minnesota. He graduated from St. Olaf College in 1949 when he was barely twenty years of age with a major in literature and philosophy, and his first intentions upon graduation were to go to sea and complete a novel he had been encouraged to write by his professors. But as the novel developed, he realized he was far too green behind the ears to meaningfully resolve the conflicts he had posed for his characters, and so he abandoned the work.

Before long, the question of what to do with his own life was settled by the outbreak of war in Korea, and the appearance in the morning's mail of a draft notice. The horrible carnage then taking place among green U. S. draftees in that conflict frightened him no end, and so, never opening his draft notice, he went and enlisted instead in the Air Force. He reasoned that four years in uniform could be like a secular monastery for him. His body would be taken care of in exchange for minimal, external acts of obedience, allowing most of his mind and all of his spirit to be free to study and ponder the things that mattered to him, like who he really was and what his life should be about, even maybe about God.

In the Air Force he was schooled in languages (Russian and Vietnamese), and during this time he met and married an interesting girl. This girl shared a like capacity for wine and beer and endless talk about religion and philosophy; marriage looked like a good way to turn that happy circumstance into a permanent arrangement. Moreover when he was with this girl his chronic loneliness seemed to recede to the wings. While on their honeymoon, he got orders to go to the Far East, so marriage was put on hold and the loneliness returned. But existential ruminations about life, religion and philosophy went on now more than ever as he found himself in isolated intelligence posts in the Far East with little to do but read and ponder, compose interminable letters to his wife, and ponder the same questions all over again.

By the end of his enlistment he had come to an unexpected conclusion: he would to go to Union Theological Seminary in New York City and learn about God, this time in great earnest. He felt drawn to Union because he had previously heard lectures there by Paul Tillich, then one of the luminaries at Union, and Reinhold Niebuhr, another world-famous figure there. But as it turned out, the experience at the seminary, even at the hand of such figures, did nothing at all for him, nothing existentially. Except for one fateful thing: while at seminary he got an assignment as part-time field worker at an unusual, avant-garde Protestant church in Greenwich Village. It was a most unlikely assignment, but one that, given his nature and inclinations, could not have better suited him: he was to hang out with the neighborhood artists and poets and sort of become the church's presence in their midst.

After seminary, he was invited to become the associate pastor of this church, to do full-time what he had been doing all along with artists and writers of the Village. It was an invitation too good to be true, one he more than gladly accepted, but only on condition he not have to be formally ordained. Ordination was something he could not give himself to. This particular church was so liberal, to put it mildly, that this stipulation mattered little to its membership. He naturally took to these full-time duties the way a moth goes to light, but as you will see, after a few more years, by the age of thirty, and despite his marriage, his life would become filled with darkness, loneliness, confusion and, to some extent, shame, a condition that fit in well enough with the locale and the people he dealt with, but not with the needs and hunger of his soul.

Once while in military service a few years earlier, he had sat in on a barracks bull session about what each of the participants there that night wanted for his life. When it came to his turn, he said that what he wanted for himself was innocence. Later one of his friends came up to him shaking his head asking why he would ever set such an impossible goal. We've all lost our innocence, the friend said. The only reply he could think of was to quote something he had read in the writings of a Russian Orthodox philosopher: *innocence is lost in life and regained in holiness.* Of course that answer only deepened the problem for he had no idea how holiness was possible for a sinner, someone who by definition, as St. Bernadette said, "loved sin." He did not know how it could ever be possible for a really sinful man to achieve holiness, but in the back of his mind he understood very well that *this* was the ultimate dilemma, at least for him, and that he for one would never be happy or peaceful until he had uncovered the way, if one existed, to be what he wasn't, to change what he didn't really want to change, and attain what he dreamt about but couldn't lift a finger to achieve. Now three years at seminary had still not disclosed it to him, and three years of unconventional ministry had made it seem more remote and unlikely than ever. This unhealthy state of mind was approaching a danger point when one day the unexpected happened, an encounter that led to the cure of all these infirmities, first the darkness and loneliness, then the confusion, finally the shame, and that changed his life forever.

Chapter Two

SEEDINGS

1

At the time I first met this man who I will simply call Doc (for that is what everyone called him in those days), I was working in Greenwich Village as an unordained Protestant minister, at a liberal church known as Judson Memorial. The church building, designed by Stanford White, is familiar for its tall, landmark Italian Renaissance campanile. In more recent years this church has achieved a certain notoriety for its radical stance on abortion and gay rights issues, among other things, but in earlier times the church was a bit tamer, more nearly what you would just call a liberal Protestant church with a typical this-world orientation, a church that modestly thought of itself as a "half-way house" for the unchurched, a stepping stone to the real church somewhere.

My role at this church was that of loosely defined missionary to the surrounding bohemian community. The idea was that if the natives would not come to the church, the church would go to them. I was to hang out and be the church in their midst. I did my job well and spent so much of my time in the streets, cafes, galleries and bars of the Village that, given the inclinations of my nature, I soon became a native myself, a true bohemian, a convert in reverse. I grew a beard and spoke the white Negro jargon of the jazz scene where money was "bread," things were "cool, man," to "dig" meant to really get it, and anyone who lived north of Fourteenth Street (i.e., north of the Village) was "out of it."

Life in the Village was pretty pagan, and a missionary from this avant-garde church was hardly expected to stand up on a soapbox and preach the Gospel. I couldn't have done that in any case. My work was more a *travail de présence*, as they used to say of the French worker-priests after the Second World War. I'm not sure what that phrase meant exactly – its appeal was that it could mean practically anything you wanted. In my case it meant red wine and late night conversation about French poets and Russian authors more than anything overtly religious, though truthfully God was never far from my mind. I wanted to be his friend and do his work in a way, but I never felt I was doing very well on either score.

Once a month, though, I had to preach a Sunday sermon to the regular congregation, a good many of whom lived north of Fourteenth Street, and so two or three days before that Sunday assignment, I would hole up in this little room I had for an office in my apartment right behind the church on Thompson Street, and sort of go on a retreat to get myself into the spirit of the thing. During these times of seclusion I would read the New Testament, existentially, like I was trying to really come to grips with this thing called Christian faith. I wanted to preach out of that faith somehow, even to this liberal congregation, and in a real way I was trying to take a stiff draught of it in preparation for my Sunday gig. I say this lightly but I took those sermons seriously. In my heart I wanted to serve God, even if the condition were, paradoxically, that I be the one to define all the terms.

The thing that always impressed me during these perusals of the New Testament, particularly as I paged through the *Acts of the Apostles* and the *Letters* of St. Paul and St. John, was how "far out" in their own way those early believers were. There was something strange about them, something I could never quite relate to from what I knew of the world. I couldn't put my finger on it exactly, but these people literally seemed to *move* in God somehow, like he was their primary element, the way water is to fish only more so because with them God was on the inside as well, in their brain cells and very marrow. Even after Jesus was gone from their midst, these disciples and early believers behaved as if he was right there with them and in them all the time. They asked things of him and he provided, as he said he would. And they gave him what *he* wanted too, like themselves and all their worldly attachments. I knew of no one in my Protestant experience who had that kind of give-and-take with God. I knew people who believed in God most genuinely, whose faith would easily put mine to shame, but even their faith was a sorry affair compared to those first believers. Jesus had said, *Without me you can do nothing.* I didn't know anybody who really believed that, who didn't act as if they were on their own 99.99 percent of the time. *Without me you can do nothing.* Who thinks he needs God to turn on a light or to deposit a check at the bank? Maybe those early Christians didn't think that way either, but I wondered about it. I remember Romano Guardini once said that you should be able to tell a Christian just by the way he or she moves. I wondered about that too. What would a person be like who believed God is present in things like headaches and telephone calls, and even in the way one picks up the receiver?

> *Could we pierce the veil and were we vigilant and attentive, God would reveal himself continuously to us and we should rejoice in his action in everything that happened to us. . . . If we lived uninterruptedly by the life of faith, we should be in continual contact with God, we should speak with him face to face. As the air is the medium for transmitting our thoughts and words to others, so all our deeds or sufferings would transmit to us the thoughts and words of God. (De Caussade, J.P.,* Self-Abandonment to Divine Providence, *p. 19.)*
>
> *A man of God should so appear and conduct himself that there would be no one who would not desire to see him, no one who would not wish to hear him, no one who, having seen him, would not believe that he was a Son of God. (St. Augustine,* On the Christian Life.*)*

I tell you this because the day Doc came to our apartment in Greenwich Village, the moment in fact that I opened the apartment door and saw this lean, gray-haired man peering at me with his luminous, dark brown eyes, I felt I was looking at someone right out of the New Testament. I do not know why I felt that, but the thought flashed through my mind the instant I saw him. And that's exactly how he was, someone straight out of those ancient times, a kind of modern day Paul who saw God in everything and everything in God, who lived with God, who did everything he did as an act of cooperation with God, who could not so much as pick up a glass of water without giving the impression that God was doing it with him. It was not a little mesmerizing, which is why after a while you could hardly take your eyes off this man.

* * *

The modern world gives every appearance of getting along perfectly well without God, but that appearance of being okay, as any honest person will tell you, is surely an illusion. Underneath, the world is a colossal mess. I knew I was a mess, deep down perhaps worse than anyone. The little world I hid away in during those monthly retreats, where I sometimes caught a taste of inner peace, and the world I moved in the rest of the time, where I had no peace, these two worlds had little to do with each other. If anything, they were foes, each with its own center of gravity, each its own god, each its own imperious claim to my body and soul. You cannot serve two masters; inevitably you will love the one and hate the other. I knew these words of Jesus were true but that didn't keep me from trying. I could not turn my back on God, but neither could I ignore this other pull of my nature. In short I was a thoroughly split person, still hoping somehow the world wouldn't notice. In my better moments I was all for God and his perfect and holy ways, but the life I lived most of the time was something quite different, something disordered and sicklied o'er with the pale cast of almost unbroken narcissism. There were times, in my better moments, when I wanted to change, to be a better person, but how do you go about *not* being the person you are? And what do you do when you are convinced that this person whom you can't do anything about is unlovable? On the inside you begin to hate yourself and on the outside you hide. Except that you can't hide so easily from God. That's when the mind starts playing its dangerous games.

Doc told me a few years later, when by then I could afford to hear such things about myself, that when he first met me I was pre-psychotic. I tell you this not to dramatize myself, but so that you may know with whom and with what God was dealing when he sent me help one fateful day. Doc was not a psychiatrist, so the diagnosis may not have been accurate, but he knew something wasn't right with me, and I knew it too.

2

God began his reclaiming work with a telephone call the morning of March 28th, 1960. My wife Terry and I had been up drinking red wine until three in the morning – it had been my 31st birthday – and we were dead asleep when the ringing woke us. I reached for the phone by the bed and cleared my voice.

–Hello.

It was my poet friend Howard Hart (we called him Howie) with his nervous laugh, usually indicating something was afoot. I looked at the clock. It was 9:50.

–What's up, Howie?

–Guess what. Doc's in town!

I felt something go dead inside.

–Oh yeah?

—Yeah, Howie echoed with a laugh. *No foolin'. He wants to come and see you.* I could only greet this with silence.

—You awake? Laughter.

—We were up pretty late last night.

More Laughter. Howie's laugh had nothing to do with something being funny.

—We'll be right over. We're just finishing breakfast. We went to the nine o'clock at Our Lady of Guadalupe. Fifteen minutes, OK?

More silence.

I was trying to work my way out of a bomb crater. I knew who Howie was talking about, of course. That was my problem. Howie had spoken to Terry and me a lot about his special friend in Mexico, and we had always said we'd really like to meet him sometime. But not this sometime, not with red wine still doing its thing in the brain. I knew enough about this Doc to know he wasn't the sort of person you want to meet without preparation. For sure not without a clear head.

—You still there?

I cleared my throat.

—Howie, we're still in bed.

Laughter.

—See you in fifteen. He hung up.

Terry had her eyes open by this time.

—What was that all about? she asked.

—Howie. His friend Doc is in town.

I lit two cigarettes and held out one for Terry.

—They're coming right over, I said. *Doc wants to meet us.*

We got out of bed and went about putting ourselves and our apartment in some kind of order. Things were a glorious mess. Terry washed up while I put the half-gallon wine jug away – it was practically on empty – and dumped out the ashtrays. There was a half-eaten birthday cake on the coffee table, something really good that Terry had baked. I left it where it was. I opened the blinds and a bright fresh morning sun came streaming in, transforming the living room. I was grateful for the effect. Then I went and threw some water on my face and dressed. I think I managed to shave too while Terry put on some coffee. Our four-year-old daughter, Sarah, had gotten up earlier on her own and was outside in the backyard, playing with her little friend from upstairs. We let her stay there, though she hadn't had breakfast far as anyone could tell. I was in a controlled state of panic, and I think Terry felt little different.

Then the doorbell rang and I went to open it. The man standing next to my friend Howie was gray-haired, thin, somewhat swarthy, of average height, fairly deep into his fifties, looking right at me with intelligent, unsettling eyes, and no trace of a smile.

I wanted him to smile at me, to meet my eyes and light up. I always looked for that when I met someone new, someone I had to become involved with in some way. It sets the mind at rest, reassures you that things will work out between you, at least be bearable if not a pleasure. It's a sign the other person will meet you half-way. I was smiling of course and extending my hand. My poet friend Howie's face was Greenwich Village beatific as he made the introductions, and in the next moment I was leading them down the long hall to the living room, feeling terribly confused. I sensed that this would be no easy meeting. I signaled for Terry to come in from the kitchen (she was lying low making coffee), made the

Seedings

introductions and got everyone seated. Howie noticed the birthday cake, which thankfully gave sudden purpose to my life. I put a plate of cake in front of our visitors and made sure of the forks. Then Terry came in with coffee, which took care of the next few moments. The visitor looked around at the room and said we had a nice apartment, nice and light. That was about all he said. I was trying to figure out what to do next when Howie picked up a manuscript lying on the coffee table. It was a sermon I had preached two days previously – one of those once-a-month sermons I mentioned earlier – and had neglected to file away. It had a red wine glass stain on the top page. I explained what it was and Howie passed it over to Doc, who began to read it. Howie and I exchanged a few words while I watched Doc out of one eye. Doc looked up from his reading and said, *I like this.* He smiled at me, went back to reading, and suddenly the morning seemed bright with possibilities.

I should say something about that sermon. The sermon was on the Parable of the Sower. In this parable Jesus told of a sower who went out to sow seeds, some of which fell by the wayside and died at once, others fell among rocks and took root, only to be starved for nourishment and die. Still other seeds were eaten by birds or strangled by weeds. Only a small part of the seeds took root in good soil and flourished. It's a favorite subject of sermons, and most preachers focus on what happens to the seed, which after all is the point of Jesus' teaching. But for some reason I wrote about the sower instead, about how this stranger went around planting seed into uncomprehending, sometimes reluctant soil. The sermon even had a dialogue between the sower and the soil. The soil wanted to know what the sower was up to, and when the sower said he was going to plant a seed that would bring forth a "lovely little flower," the soil told him not to waste his time: *We're meant for potatoes*, the soil said. *If we're meant for flowers like you say, how come others don't know about it?* The sower replied: *These others don't know because I have not yet come to them. But today I've come to you.*

The visitor put the sermon down and nodded that it was really very sweet. Then he reached into the inner pocket of his sport jacket and took out an envelope and a pen. There was some writing on the back of the envelope. *I started to write something during my meditation after Mass*, he said. *Let me see if I can finish it. Maybe there'll be something in this for you.* He read what he had written in silence and then closed his eyes like he was praying, or thinking on some really deep level. Then he opened his eyes and began to write. This meditative process went on for maybe five minutes. when finally he looked over at Terry and me and asked if we would like to hear what he had written. We of course sat forward, all ears. It was short, maybe only six or eight sentences or so. The lines were written as if Jesus had spoken them himself. I only remember the first sentence, and it has stuck in my memory ever since:

This is my will for you that you should have my joy.

Doc looked at us and smiled. *Maybe this is for you,* he said. Terry and I shook our heads up and down, not knowing quite what to make of it. Howie went into his jazz poet's ecstasy and said, *Wow!* All I could think of was something stupid like, *I sure hope so.*

It was so weird. Within ten or fifteen minutes, with hardly anything being said, this stranger had already begun to shift the ground beneath our feet. I couldn't figure out what was happening. We had hardly met and here we were, beyond small talk, beyond serious ideas even, touching on a matter so deep one hardly knew how to formulate it. Except that we felt it was something good, possibly even momentous. What was so strange was that I half-believed these words had actually come from God, not this man.

Terry and I had such deep misgivings about God. I for one wanted to be his friend, to love Him, to belong to Him, but hardly anything I did, said, or thought really served that end. Most of what passed for my day, and the long nights, should have turned God against me, if my conscience were any measure. I'm sure it was no different with Terry. But now, in the space of those twenty minutes, a strange new notion would begin its long hard journey into my mind and heart: Our relationship to God isn't something that rests in *our* hands exactly, something we are obliged to pull off on our own somehow; no, it was something God does. Oddly enough, that was exactly what I had preached about the previous Sunday only I hadn't connected with it personally. Now I began to half-glimpse that my relationship to God, the one I worried about all the time, would sprout of itself from a seed that God himself gets around to planting. It was still far less than half an idea at this point, but in those first minutes in that living room that morning, I felt the strong thrust of a spade breaking through bedrock deep in my soul. It seemed truly wondrous and painful all at the same time.

The blade struck a buried object and I did an unexpected thing. I stood up suddenly and said there was something I needed to get. I went to my little office off our bedroom and dug out a stack of thick loose-leaf notebooks. These were some journals, thick half-musty volumes of meditations that I had kept during my tour in the Air Force some years earlier. I found what I was looking for in one of them and took it back into the other room. *There's something I'd like to show you*, I said, handing Doc an opened notebook. On the page was a tiny handwritten poem I had penned while stationed at Clark Field in the Philippines. It was dated sometime in the summer of 1953. I had never shown it to anyone before in my life. Why was I doing this now?

It was hardly a poem, as poems go, but it said much about its author. The pathetic part is that the person it addresses existed only in its author's mind, like a wish.

> The kiss of your prayer for me
>   is closer than your lips
>   more actual than your breath.
> When you whisper my name before God
>   you become mine
>   more than I can dream.
> As for me, dear friend,
>   I am only yours
>   the moment I am first all His.

I don't know what made me think of that little piece just then; it had lain in my notebooks half-forgotten for eight years. Probably it was that mention of joy: *This is my will for you that you should have my joy.* What kind of gift would that be? How would it fit in with what I wanted

Seedings

for myself? I needed to know. If supernatural promise and simple human desire were incompatible, if they were at odds with each other as I secretly feared, where would that leave me? I know I stopped breathing as our visitor read my little poem, but I need not have been anxious. Something stirred in him at once and I could tell that he liked it. It was a pivotal moment that flicked by almost without a word. But somewhere a door had flung open. God had not said NO to me or so it seemed just then—after only twenty minutes in this man's presence I was already taking his reactions as signs.

Only later would I realize how much this man himself was driven by a need to put human love and divine love together, to experience them as one and the same somehow, as if the heart could not tolerate two separate and unrelated loves, neither of which the heart could do without. As he saw it, there are no soloists in heaven. That's how Jesus saw it too: *Where two or three are gathered in my Name, there am I in their midst.* Of course *being gathered in his Name* will mean different things to different people. As I came to learn, to Doc it could only mean *union.* Joy was union with another in God. Joy was union with God in another. I was far from understanding it, nor did Doc allude to it on that occasion, but something far down in my nature took comfort that morning. God had answered a question that had lain within me unasked since early manhood, like a sleeping animal. Unasked I am sure because I was too afraid of the answer. Perhaps I always knew the answer but doubted that it would ever be for me. The unspoken response I got that morning went through me like a deep comforting electric shock, if such a thing is possible, or maybe like a first installment on that promise given to us moments earlier, for in that brief instant I tasted joy. Looking back, I think that fleeting thrill was the moment when scattered seed fell to ground, for everything that would happen after this, through the labors of this man, would happen now under the rubric of human nature taking root and growing, and one fine day finding its fulfillment in overwhelming joy. And as it turned out it was always more than I could dream, always.

Allow me to digress for a moment and present some of Doc's own poems, written many years before my first meeting with him. These pieces will let you understand the man on this matter of the heart better than I could hope to do. In his case the woman in the poems was a real person, the wife of his early years.

> Oh my lady!
> This love that I bear you
>   is not mine
> For I know that it is without limit
> And if you do feel for one single
>   moment
> The power of this not-mine love
> You too must know that it is not
>   your own.
> And yet, lovely lady, all that is mine to
>   give is given:
> For I cannot give all, but giving all,
> Must give what is beyond mine own
>   possession.
> Therefore such is the force of my love,

> That by it God is invoked to smile
>   upon it
> And in His pleasure it is both ours
>   and His.

And again:
> If, most lovely lady,
> The soft precise avowal of your eyes
> Was something given, as if by your
>   dear self,
> Then, even the strong assurance of
>   those selfless lips
> Would not assure our love among
>   eternal things.
> But knowing in what is known
>   through them
> That they, mortal eyes and lips,
> Do not convey their own intention,
> There is certainty, and their loveliness
>   transformed.

When I was in the Air Force studying the Russian language at Syracuse University – this was when I was single – I met a woman in a bar one evening. She was unhappily married and happened to go to this bar that evening out of lonely desperation, hoping to meet someone. By chance she met another lonely soul and we sort of became friends. Over the next couple of weeks we spoke on the telephone a lot and meet three or four times in a bar to talk and I became rather drawn to her. We talked about making love too but it was not what I was really looking for and so nothing much happened on that score. But what ended it, when we were together

The Man I Called Father

talking one Saturday night, was my suggestion that we both go to some church the next morning. She looked at me like I was stark raving mad. It was of course an insane idea. But not the urge to bring even scraggy love to love's Source, to take that first step, that it might be transformed somehow, however pitiable the circumstance.

Here's another of Doc's poems, about human love when human love is restored to its Source.

> The smile of my beloved,
>   O my Jesus,
> Whispers Your joy to me.
> Because my beloved
> Knows You are she
> Loved by me,
> Because my beloved
> Knows You are she
> Loving me.
> The smile of my beloved,
>   O my Jesus,
> Whispers "This is He
> Loving me!"

3

After those brief exchanges that first morning, Doc got up and said he had to leave but that, if we liked, he would come back to see us the next day. I walked him and my friend Howie outside and went down the street with them to the corner on Third and Thompson. We shook hands, and as he held my hand he drew me to himself, or tried to, because I resisted. *I think we're going to be friends*, he said, looking straight at me. *I hope so*, I said a bit weakly. This time it was I who didn't smile.

You must understand that this was hardly a case of love at first sight. Meeting this Doc was exhilarating to say the least but not a little unnerving too. What kind of man was this? We actually hadn't really exchanged a single idea, just a few more or less friendly words, and those bits of writing. There was something marvelous and inviting about him, no doubt about it, but at the same time I had this feeling I had just walked into an iron fence. I was afraid that my life was about to run out of room. It wasn't a good life, I could hardly argue that, but it was *my* life after all and I wanted to go on living it my way. I was not about to let some stranger move in and tell me something different, no matter how fascinating he might be. I saw enough in thirty minutes to realize this man was extremely dangerous.

If a seed had indeed been planted that morning, this soil was about to resist.

My wife Terry had not joined us on the street. She had said practically nothing the whole time, yet in her quiet way she had come to her own conclusions about this mystery man. The truth is this strange visitation may have been more for her than anyone.

The next day around noon I went up to 27th Street to see an art printer. I was publishing an *avant garde* literary magazine in those days called *Exodus* and I had to check galley proofs of some drawings by two artists that I was planning to include in a forthcoming issue. One of the artists, Claes Oldenberg, was a good friend, and the other, Red Grooms, a bare acquaintance – two young artists my own age more or less just getting started in those days, though today both are world-class figures. When I finished my business on 27th Street it was a little past two o'clock. Howie had telephoned earlier that he and Doc would be at our place at two, so they would be there by now. I lived on Thompson between Third and Fourth Streets, and could easily have taken a cab or a bus and been home in a matter of minutes. Instead I walked, though I never walked distances like that as a rule. I was obviously in no hurry to get home. I walked so slowly it took me fully forty minutes and in that time I entertained a surging stream of second thoughts about this man Doc, most of which were outright hostile.

When I finally entered our apartment, by now feeling a little guilty for these thoughts, I was relieved to find things seemed to have gotten on quite well without me. Doc was at the piano and Terry was seated next to him. For some reason Howie wasn't there. As I came in Doc looked over at me with an expression that told me he knew exactly what I had been up to; but it wasn't a judging look, just a look of truth. And somehow I *knew* he knew about those second thoughts. Then he turned back to the keyboard. He was into a Beethoven sonata, as I recall, and Terry sat there beside him utterly absorbed. I sat back and slowly began to relax. Indeed I became quite peaceful.

I ask the reader to put yourself in my shoes for a moment. You have just met a formidable individual about whom you feel terribly ambivalent. The person commands your attention, almost uncomfortably so, and you find yourself uneasy over this authority he seems to have, over what he thinks of you, what he may say to you about yourself. He's an impressive person and you, in turn, would like to hold your own, but he doesn't seem easily impressed. You are frankly a little scared of him and not a little annoyed at having to contend with this new and unwanted factor in your life. You think all kinds of thoughts to justify why you should keep him out of your life. Some of your thoughts are frankly hostile. You find yourself trying to put these thoughts away as you prepare to greet him. You smile and you try some small talk. You are gracious, eager to prove your civility, your intelligence, suddenly eager to prove (even to yourself) that you do like this person. But something goes wrong. You realize he doesn't play that game. You realize that he has read your mind, that he knows very well what you have been thinking for the past hour. And who can guess what else he might realize about you. Your act is blown. In such circumstances, how would anyone feel? Unsettled? No doubt. But it wasn't that way with me at all.

How can I explain to you what took place in those few seconds, beginning with my *knowing that he knew* and ending with that first wave of peace? In that briefest of intervals I went through something that I had never experienced before: a sense of having been turned inside out, for just the briefest instant of having been *seen* for what I really was, and of having survived quite nicely. And then almost immediately this unexpected sense of peace. The episode hadn't unsettled me, wrecked my afternoon, ruined my relationship with this man. Just the opposite, it seemed to create the basis for the beginnings of one. This man of God had somehow *read my mind* and let it pass. There was no judgment, just truth and knowledge, and quiet acceptance, not rejection. And an aftermath in which I felt peaceful and free to be the person he saw in me, the person I couldn't accept in myself.

If you who are reading this narrative have a healthy psyche, all of this may strike you as much ado about nothing. A healthy soul hardly blinks when truth flashes its light on it. Indeed, the healthy soul grows uneasy should that light ever go out. But there was little in me that could be called healthy. As a Protestant youth I never looked at myself – let alone revealed myself – the way a Catholic youth learns to do in the minutes before entering a confessional. My solution to everything wrong in me was to put on a mask and keep to the shadows. No doubt such masks are worn in confessionals too, but like a shrewd priest, this man that afternoon had the grace to see through mine and the experience left me feeling as cleansed as if I had made a good confession, albeit it in this case one mediated by a single look. That afternoon, joy's second installment came, as I said, on a wave of peace. I now think of that episode as the moment when a seedling's tiny tendril won a small victory over hard soil and finally took root.

This was the first of many, many such healing moments at the hands of this Doc – a man with singular grace to see through souls that have been given to him for this purpose – moments of truth, some of them eventually hard and even bloody, but always bringing us closer to what God had intended when he fashioned us, and always ending in deepening peace. It would never be easy for me: the notion that the truth was my friend was something I for one would have great difficulty believing, and would have to learn and re-learn again and again, and am still learning – that the truth brings good in its wake, not undoing, that moments of truth such as I experienced that morning are God's opportunities, one of his ways of drawing us, and his ways are always merciful. I am learning and re-learning this even as I write these pages.

How strong and un-uprootable in us remains that ancient impulse of our first parents to cope with guilt by turning from the truth and hiding!

Our apartment was on the street level, and it was an unusually warm day that afternoon in late March, so the floor-to-ceiling windows of our living room were wide open. From where I sat I could see that several black men had stopped on the sidewalk outside and were listening to the piano. I recognized one of them, a local drug dealer who had been a hip jazz musician at one point in his life. The other two looked to be junkies already a little stoned. The dealer caught my eye and broke into a big smile: *All right!* he said, his whole body suddenly come alive. *I like that. Who's making that sound? A friend of mine*, I shouted back through the window after some hesitation. *He's alll rrright. Hey, man, can I come in? Let me come in. I got to catch this man.* By this time, Doc had turned around and was looking at me quizzically. He could see the small mottled audience on the sidewalk outside our window. *Hey, just me, man*, the dealer called through the window. *Just for a minute. I got to catch this. I ain't gonna cause no trouble.* Doc looked at me as if to say it was OK with him if it was OK with me. I nodded and found myself opening the door to a junkie I would normally not have wanted in my home under any circumstances, all at the instigation of a man who only yesterday himself walked through the door a perfect stranger. I wasn't sure I liked what was happening but it certainly wasn't dull. The jazz musician/drug dealer in fact didn't stay long and his behavior was impeccable. Doc was very kind to him and played as if for him specially. The man first sat rather tentatively on a straightback chair but soon got up and stood over the piano, his black streetwise face lit up with pleasure. I found myself delighting in the scene too, in its incongruity, and in the music. Doc's playing was unmistakably in a class by itself. It wasn't exactly polished, in the way that a performance is polished. He played from a score Terry had given him, and he often went back over a part, like he was practicing, searching for something, sometimes playing a single measure repeatedly until he got what he wanted. You could hear what he was after and it always made superb musical sense. There was something in the way he made the music talk that grabbed you, like voices speaking to one another, and to you. He used to say later it all had to do with musical wit, voices conversing with each other, sometimes playfully, sometimes lovingly, sometime sorrowfully, but always with articulated intelligence. You could tell this was no ordinary kind of playing. I know this now about Doc's playing from the vantage point of later years and countless hours spent by his side at the piano. The jazz musician knew it from the few measures he caught though an open window as he and his buddies strolled by. Terry knew it better than any for she seemed utterly lost in what Doc was doing at the keyboard.

Terry was then (and remains today) a serious musician, not terribly accomplished as a performer, though devoted to both the piano and the cello. Her real calling was composition, but it was not something that she did very much of in those days, except perhaps in the secret recesses of her mind. She had a kind of genius for composition but it would not fully come to light until many years later, even though the signs of it were already there. Not long before Doc came into our lives, she had written the incidental music and songs for an off–off Broadway play that I had produced. The play was a modern adaptation of Goethe's *Faust.* and was directed by Chuck Gordone, a black friend of ours who would one day go on to win a Pulitzer prize for a play of his own. The production itself was more or less a non-event but the few critics who paid it any attention had only good words for Terry's music.

Later that afternoon, as Doc was getting ready to leave, he took me aside and confided to me something Terry had whispered while sitting by him at the piano. *Take me away from all this,* she had said to him. I was really dumbstruck, as if the flooring had given way beneath me. I suppose I knew that Terry felt that way about our life together in the Village; I felt that way myself much of the time. But it was another thing having others know it, especially someone important whom you wanted to impress. Terry, bless her heart, had just stepped on my narcissistic big toe. But her quiet, honest desperation pried open a door, one with a huge exit sign hung over it, and before much longer, pretenses gone by now, we would all dash through that opening to a new life. Had Terry felt differently about this man, had she sought to incorporate him as just one more interesting facet in the existing order of things, the way I was wont to do, it's quite possible I wouldn't be writing this story now. In a real way I owe my sanity to her desperation. So strangely does God work his ways—eternal destinies woven by delicate tendrils intertwined in ways we will only understand in another life.

We saw Doc every day after that for about a week, during which I gradually became more comfortable with him, and then he returned to Mexico where he had been living for the past few years. Before he took his leave, a strange thing happened. We were alone in our apartment, Doc, Terry and I, and Doc was getting ready to go. We had grown much closer during the week and we wanted to see him again. We were expressing these sentiments when he suddenly looked at Terry and said *I have something for you.* He opened his valise and rummaged about for a moment until he found what it was he wanted. *I think this is meant for you,* he said, handing Terry a plain pewter crucifix with wooden inlay, a little on the large size. *I took this off the wall by my bed just as I was leaving to come up here. I think Jesus wants you to have this.* As he passed it to Terry it fell to the floor. Terry seemed flabbergasted. Soon as Doc left, she told me she had been praying for a crucifix and now she had just been handed one. The episode blew her mind and left a deep impression on me too. Her words brought back to mind another episode involving Terry and a crucifix. This happened eight years previously, when Terry and I were just beginning to really get to know each other. I was in the Air Force, stationed in Washington, DC, studying Vietnamese at a top-secret government agency, and I used to come to Brooklyn every third weekend or so to be home with my parents who lived in Bay Ridge, and to see Terry, who lived a bus ride away in Flatbush, within sound of Ebbets Field. One Saturday night, Terry and I were drinking beer at a back table in a neighborhood bar. We had been talking philosophy and religion all evening and suddenly, *apropos* of nothing, I looked at her and said, *You know what I would really like to have? A crucifix.* Terry let out a little cry, reached into her purse and handed me a small pewter crucifix with wooden inlay, wrapped in a paper napkin. *I saw it in a pawn shop window this afternoon and bought it for you*, she said. It was exactly like the one she would receive from Doc, only much smaller. I put it on my dog chain and never took it off until it literally fell apart some years later.

Doc went back to Mexico and our lives returned to normal (in the loosest sense of that word). One of the first things we did was to get together with Howie for a *post-mortem* on Doc's visit. We learned some interesting things. Doc had confided to Howie that he had come up to New York at this time because he felt there was someone here in the Northeast that God wanted him to meet. Someone important. He thought it was a woman. That revelation was a little mind-blowing. Howie also said that Doc had already known about me from an earlier trip to New York. On that earlier visit, Howie had shown him a sermon of mine that had been published in the *Village Voice*, at that time a local, *avant garde* Greenwich Village newspaper rather different from what it was to become later. The sermon was entitled *Waiting for God*, and was announced boldly as the headline across the top of the front page. The title was a play on Beckett's *Waiting for Godot*, which was being performed in New York around that time, but the sermon itself was only incidentally about the play. It was chiefly about the phenomenon of waiting and about how the Jews had taught the world the habit of waiting. I contrasted the Jewish attitude about time and history to other cultures in the world, particularly the Greeks, who saw time and history as an inferior part of nature, locked into nature's cyclicality. It was the Jews with their hope for the Messiah who taught us that history was above nature and would bring something new and unrepeatable into the world to which even nature would be subject. To those ancient faithful Jews, this waiting for the appearance of the Messiah in the fullness of time was the very heart of their spirituality. They were the only people of whom that could be said to be true. So waiting is quintessentially Jewish, I argued.

I tried to illustrate the Jewishness of waiting with an experience I once had upon walking into Prospect Park in Brooklyn one warm sunny afternoon. This park is actually quite huge, but the section of the park I visited was located in Flatbush, a predominantly Jewish part of Brooklyn, a few blocks from where Terry lived. As I walked into the park that afternoon, I noticed how all the benches by the entrance were jammed up with middle-aged and elderly Jews, mostly men, with not a single empty seat. The benches a few hundred feet beyond the entrance were almost empty, and those a few hundred yards further on, facing the water of a lovely lake, were entirely vacant. This is where I took a seat, looking out on the water. Why would these Jews prefer to sit by the busy park entrance, so close to the street and the exhaust fumes of the traffic and the buses that stood there idling, when there was this lovely lake to contemplate? Then I remembered Biblical accounts of Jewish elders sitting by the city gates, and realized that Jews have been sitting by gates and entrances to public places for over twenty-five centuries. Were they awaiting news of the Promised One? Did they expect that the Messiah himself might just suddenly come into view one day, walking down some dusty road of history? I think it must be so. I tell you I could not help noticing when I came into the park how many Hebrew eyes rose to study the face of a stranger, this stranger, as I passed. It was usually only the briefest of glances, but there was something questioning, probing in it, utterly different from the way *goyim* look at you, if they look at you at all. These Jews were just doing what their people had been doing for centuries, or so it seemed to me. To be sure, the Jews there that afternoon were waiting because of what was in their bones, not their heads, or even their hearts perhaps. If you went up to one of the men and asked him if he was waiting for the Messiah, he'd look at you like you were *meshuga*. But it didn't matter. The habit was in them. Jews are a people who have been taught to wait, and I concluded that in the measure Christian *goyim* look for the Second Coming of Christ, our waiting, too, was something learned from Jews.

Howie told me that when Doc read this sermon he said if he ever met me he would convert me to the Church. He said he would show me how to find Christ here and now, not in some future coming. Doc, for all his Jewishness, was above all a mystic, Hellenist as much as Hebrew. For him, like those early Christians, faith today is not to *wait* for God but to *see* God, in everything, here and now.

We got a little note from Doc towards the middle of April. He told us he had gone to the Easter Vigil midnight Mass at the Basilica of Our Lady of Guadalupe in Mexico City, and that in taking Communion he had received Jesus especially for us. He said he would be coming back to New York soon and would like to stay with us for a while.

Meanwhile our life in the Village went on pretty much as before.

4

Allow me now to tell you some things about that life in Greenwich Village. I start out with some of the more or less positive exterior things, to give you a feeling for how I spent my time, and then progress from there to a more inward look. In what follows, I can only speak for myself, not for Terry

As part of my so-called "missionary" activities, I had started an art gallery called the *Judson Gallery* in a suite of basement rooms directly beneath our apartment. The gallery had a walk-down entrance off the street outside our windows and almost immediately became a center of activity. I developed a friendship with two painters in particular who would later go on to become world-famous artists: Claes Oldenburg and Jim Dine. Claes and I became good friends and for a while we saw each other almost every day. Judson Gallery also put on some of the first "happenings" in New York, involving Allan Kaprow, the inventor of that unusual art form.

Tom Wesselmann was another acquaintance and

one of our earliest exhibitors. Many of these artists had their first New York show in this gallery and some of them, like Claes and Jim Dine, were intimately involved in making the gallery a happening in its own right. In fact, the art movement of the Sixties, famous for its turning from abstract expressionism back to representational (albeit often dadaist) images, can be said to have had one of its beginnings in this gallery.

Claes Oldenburg, Jim Dine, another artist by the name of Marc Ratliff, and I were in the gallery late one Saturday afternoon. We had just closed Jim Dine's one-man show and were sitting on the floor with our backs against the walls beneath Jim's paintings, wondering what to do next when I suddenly had a thought. Let's have a group show, I said, and suggested some ideas for it. For the next few hours we let our imaginations play freely. The notion I was intuitively working with was that of the interpenetration of art and reality. I suggested to Jim Dine that he create a painting that you could walk inside of. It was a long, spontaneous but somehow reflective meeting during which something seemed to gel. Anyway, one thing led to another and before long we opened a show called *Ray Gun Specs* and it had a painting by Jim that was literally a room you entered. On the outside, it looked like a small square hut that some homeless person might have put together under the Brooklyn Bridge, but inside all was three dimensional space packed densely with a plethora of painted objects, some found, some made, all essentially just junk, hanging from the ceiling, projecting from the walls and floor, blended with special lighting, and out from which emitted a flow of spontaneous sounds and meaningless utterances from a tape recording we had all contributed to. It wasn't particularly memorable, actually, just junk like old boots and such arranged and painted to take on the properties of art. Claes' work in the exhibit was a scene of life-size paper maché figures and objects (a "paperbag bum", a fire hydrant, street litter) plus his wife (in the flesh) done up in painted burlap bags stooping among the litter. It was all done in flowing ribbons and patches of gray and white paint bathed in an eerie lighting.

This notion of a painting that was "entered" gave Jim Dine another idea. In conjunction with the Ray Gun Specs exhibit itself, Allen Kaprow organized an evening of so-called "happenings" or "performances" to be put on by this little band of artists. I was even encouraged to do something but I couldn't get with it for some reason. Jim's idea for his own "performance" was to come on like a painter, dressed in beret and smock, and go up to this huge canvas and start to paint humming some zany song. As he worked, his motions would become more and more agitated until he flips out and begins tossing pots of paint onto the canvas, and then over himself. Finally he leaps forward and dives into the canvas. That's exactly what Jimmy did twice in one evening and the small crowds that took in his performances that night went wild. Years later, quite by chance, I heard him describe this scene during an interview on public radio.

The confusion of art and reality that underlay this *Ray Gun* exhibit, and that Jim Dine parodied in his performance, all seems rather amusing in retrospect. But the notion seemed to trigger a genuine impulse in these painters. Some time after I became a Catholic and left the scene, Allen Kaprow approached the church about their carrying on with the Judson Gallery. A painting, he told the church's representatives, was "not something you look at but something you enter." I am not sure he or any one of us at the time could have explained to on-lookers what that notion really meant. It was just the way it was in Greenwich Village and such places in those days – artists and poets with their coteries looking for meaning in the most unlikely places, like in a pair of painted boots, seeking to uncover mystery in a consumer world that had stamped mystery out, and sort of finding hints of mystery in its refuse, like crumbs from the table of an era long, long ago when everything was colored with wonder. At the time, I took all this quite seriously. I can't say I do any longer.

Behind this restless activity, speaking for myself, was a spiritual hunger, a *need* really, for something more satisfying than what I had seen of the world thus far, secular or religious. What I was looking for would not be supplied by art and poetry, of course, though in those days I somehow believed these things might help, along with many of my generation. The so-called religious people I knew – not all, but most – often seemed like the living dead, buried in middle-class banality, and I wanted no part of it except of course for the salary I faithfully drew each month. Today I would put the matter quite differently, as I trust these pages will have made clear: what was wrong with my world in those days was *me*.

My one real passion then was for writing. I was not particularly successful at it, except in a few minor instances, but in the background of almost everything I did lay a boyhood dream of becoming an important writer. Around the time I met Doc, I was working on a book of prose poems bearing the title *The Pseudepigrapha of St. Blue*. I was going to claim that I had found these pieces quite by chance at the back of a closet in an empty apartment on the Lower East Side, real author unknown. These pieces are lost now but I still remember two of them, given on the following page.

Around this time I also started an *avant garde* literary quarterly called *Exodus*. The magazine was funded by the heiress of the Lilly pharmaceutical fortune, who at the time was a local Village resident I had gotten to know. This woman many years later was to astound the literary world by bequeathing 100 million dollars to *Poetry* magazine. Our funding of course was peanuts compared to that, barely enough for three issues, but the publication surprisingly made an immediate impression and today is a collectors' item. (I am even told it had been included in a retrospective exhibition at the Whitney Museum, on display in a glass case.) One had to read between the lines to glean what it was we were seeking deliverance from in this magazine. There was nothing overtly religious about it, despite its title and the fact that its editor was an ersatz Protestant minister. And indeed there were pieces that could be considered scandalous to conventional mentality, but the magazine had a religious preoccupation nevertheless that was hardly concealed. Today it would be surprising for a so-called "little" magazine to have such spiritual undertones, but in those days it seemed to fit in easily with the soul-searching mood in places like Greenwich Village.

The magazine attracted a fair amount of attention in

Seedings

A BOY'S BLUE EYES
What
was there
to do, then,
when I was five
and those gypsies
with their cruel stiletto
dies stole into my room
to pierce a boy's
blue eyes the
shape of
woman

NEW YORK APOCALYPSE
I dreamt the bomb went
off last night. The Biggie. But this
really great thing happened first. Just as the
bomb comes flaming down across the sky above
the Bronx, this angel bops out from a roof hutch on
the lower East Side, grabs the bugger and
swallows it. Quick as that.
The bomb went off
but the angel
lasted one
second
longer
than
the
bomb
which
was enough

its brief life, and was described in one newspaper editorial as "not *beat* but definitely far out," meaning that the magazine was not seen as part of the "beat" movement, but that in its own way it took its stance on the fringes so to speak. That was always taken as a compliment in the circles I moved in — to be seen as outside the mainstream was a virtue. Just to give you an idea of that mentality: I grew a beard in my early Village days in order to be different, and then, one night a year or two later, when I went to a local party and found that all the men had beards, I went home and shaved mine. Being yourself meant being different.

Perhaps the tone of the magazine can best be caught in a few of the prose poems we published of the French poet Max Jacob, a Jewish convert to Catholicism. My poetry editor and friend, Howie Hart, translated these little pieces from the French with what has always struck me as genuine poetic skill.

Public Notice
A BEAUTIFUL SOUL
BRAND NEW
HAS BEEN LOST.
WILL YOU KINDLY
RETURN IT TO GOD
WHO IS ITS OWNER

Little Diary of Life in the World
Monday. Wonderful time yesterday at Melanie's, really wonderful. Marvelous.
Tuesday. Great last night with Suzanne, so much

fun. Marcel is delicious. That Anne-Marie is terrible. Impossible.

Wednesday. Very nice seeing Jules again, at his place. Maurice's paintings are charming, they really are. Don't think anything of Louis's music. Wish I could, but it's nothing, really.

Thursday.

Friday. Alfred killed himself. He was an idiot. An idiot.

Saturday. Received this note: "Will we see you tomorrow at the same place? Max has gone away to the Benedictines. What a dope."

Sunday. Must say again that Max is a dope. A little religion is all right but he is fanatical. He is. Going to the Benedictines is just plain crazy. Really.

Christian Families

Something terrific happened at the school run by monks of the Congregation of X. A miracle in fact. One monk hit a boy who was making fun of him. The boy called on Christ as witness that he wasn't making fun of him, and the white marble statue put out its arm and blessed the boy, then slapped his accuser. The monk apologized. Everyone in the class got on his knees. Vocations sprang up and do you know what happened? The families were "shocked." They pulled the boys out of school not because the teachers were hitting the students, but because the education was "much too mystical."

Unfortunately, almost simultaneously with the appearance of our first issue of *Exodus*, Leon Uris's novel of the same name hit the bookstores and became an instant bestseller. It upset us at first but the respective readerships were so different no one seemed to notice the confusion. Conceivably it even helped us. *Exodus* was great fun and the quality of writing, poetry and artwork was actually quite good. Dan Wolfe was co-editor, Howard Hart (my friend, Howie) was poetry editor, and Marc Ratliff was art editor. Dan was the co-founder (along with Norman Mailer) and editor of the *Village Voice* newspaper; Howie was a poet of considerable skill and sensitivity (Jacques Maritain had called him the "best Catholic poet writing in English today"); Marc was a gifted young artist who afterwards made it big as a designer in the New York commercial art world.

Launching a "little magazine" had its unexpected obstacles, chief of which was the difficulties in getting it circulated. Circulation is usually so small that distributors don't want to bother, especially with unknown start-ups operating on a shoestring as ours obviously was. Financially such magazines are almost always losing propositions. I heard of one lone distributor in the East, out of New Jersey, who handled "little magazines." I got in touch with him, and not long afterwards he came by in a station wagon filled with bundles of every variety of little magazine imaginable, some recognizable like *Partisan Review*, most unheard of. It was clear he worked hard for a living. He explained he was already over-committed and couldn't take on any more business, but after some persuading he agreed to take 300 copies on a one-shot basis. Hoping for more success than that, I printed 1500 copies of our first issue. It wasn't long, however, before this distributor came back asking for additional copies, first a few hundred more, than five hundred more. Finally he wanted 5000 more. More people than we had dared dream of were picking *Exodus* off the literary magazine rack in cubbyhole bookstores all over the country. Unfortunately for us we could not supply the demand: the typographer's lead had been melted down right after the first printing. No matter, it cost us more to produce the magazine than we could sell it for. *Exodus* couldn't last very long on that basis, and it didn't, though the immediate cause for the quarterly's demise was not finances but my sudden departure from the scene after the third issue.

Five or six years later, the noted Catholic poet Brother Antoninus came to visit Doc at a place where a few of us were living with him. This brother was based in a monastery somewhere out West and had come East to meet Doc and take council with him on some personal matter. As a few of us were lounging about one evening entertaining our guest during his wait for Doc's attention, someone happened to mention *Exodus* and Brother Antoninus volunteered that as far as he was concerned, *Exodus* had been the best little magazine in its day to come out of the East, and that he had just been getting around to submitting some of his poetry to it when the quarterly was discontinued. His jaw literally fell when he learned that the editor and publisher of this publication was sitting right across from him. He immediately came over and shook my hand and said he respected what I was trying to do with the magazine. Then he said something really interesting: *You kept trying to get those two things together.* I have always appreciated the sensitivity of that remark, for it was true – much of what appeared in its pages smacked of both worlds, of divine grace and human desire, two worlds not recoiling from each other but reaching out, despite the disorders of the one. I think others too may have been drawn to this magazine because of its special take on things. Later after I had left the scene, I was told that one subscriber, the head of the philosophy department at Boston College, when informed that the magazine had folded, wrote back that *Exodus* was "too good to be true." I tell you this to show, if it needs to be shown, the search in my own heart that underlay these literary efforts, and the fact that in this quest I had more company than I suspected. Perhaps you too count yourself among those for whom this issue is no idle matter.

Naturally I included some of my own work in *Exodus*. When I was trying to put the first issue of this magazine to bed, it seemed too skimpy and in need of more material, particularly another short story. Not liking any of those I had been getting through the mail, I decided to write one myself. The story was entitled *The Dolls* and sort of wrote itself as I sat in the gallery one Saturday afternoon. To my surprise this story was very well received and even won honorable mention in one of Macmillan's annual *Best Short Stories*. I got letters inviting submissions from fiction editors of big-time magazines like *Esquire*, and even an offer to handle my work by the British international literary agent Cherbonnier who handled writers like the British author Somerset Maughan, the French writer André Maurois, and the at-the-time famous American author Ben Hecht. Invitations like these are the stuff dreams are made of for aspiring unknowns, but as it happened, I never replied to these letters because just around that time a man called Doc entered my life and I had other things to think about.

I take the liberty of reproducing *The Dolls* below. As a piece of short fiction it is probably interesting enough in its own right, but I include it chiefly for what it will tell you about its author. Anyone even remotely versed in modern psychology will recognize the difficult, Kafkaesque father-son relationship that pervades the piece. Like Kafka's *Metamorphosis*, it too has a father who is depicted as disinterested and uncaring, a well-intending but yielding mother who always sides with the father, a sympathetic but inconstant sister, and the pathetic son, the centerpiece character, pictured as victim of an oversensitive nature and a family's fitful indifference. The story reflects a childhood (my own) seen through troubled eyes, and as such commits gross injustices to all parties concerned. And in common with almost all modern fiction writers, I make the hero out to be a victim, and of course an innocent one. At the time I wrote the story I did not think of the hero as myself, but the psychological motor driving the story is obvious enough.

The Dolls

At first no one thought anything of it at all to see Walter playing with his sister's dolls. She was older and had already lost interest in them. Walter was only four. When a family friend or two finally commented about it, the family agreed it was in fact rather cute of Walter to show this much affection for his sister's dolls. But the family had difficulty finding the humor others saw when Walter, by now almost six, asked the department store Santa for a doll with real hair for Christmas. That year Walter got an air rifle, a drum and an Erector set.

Walter continued to prefer dolls. He made an unusual demonstration when the sister and mother tried to take them from him. It's time you learn the ways of a man, pronounced the father, locking the dolls away. For the next three Saturdays the father took Walter out into the woods to shoot squirrels, sparrows, and Coca-Cola bottles. Walter was not an outdoorsman, and the father returned to passing Saturdays with his cronies and soon forgot the whole matter. The mother became engrossed in the quilt she was making for her daughter's hope chest, and the sister did her lessons, and they too soon forgot the matter.

There was some family comment when one day Walter came down to breakfast with his pillow trussed in the middle and a tassel cap on top. The family saw a doll in this device at once. That very day the father bought Walter a new chemistry set, and for three or four evenings thereafter the family gathered together in the basement while first the father, then the mother and the sister, made laboratory oxygen. The tiny explosions they were able to produce made everyone giggle. Walter, they agreed, after he failed to repeat the experiment, was still a little young. He may be a chemist one day, the father prophesied to the family, leaving Walter to his chemistry.

They gradually forgot the matter and did not seem to notice that Walter never went into the basement. From time to time, in family conversations with friends, the remark would be repeated.

Walter may be a chemist one day.

Walter started school and no one gave another thought to the matter until the family was summoned by his teacher for a conference. Your son is doing fairly well, she said, but there are a few things I want to speak with you about. Walter does not play with the other children, she explained. In fact he keeps entirely to himself. Walter is shy, the mother replied. Of course, the teacher said. He'll get over that. He draws a good deal of the time, she went on, producing a file with Walter's name neatly typed on it. She took out some childish scribblings. They're actually fairly well done, the teacher went on, passing them to the family. Figure studies, it seems, she said. Dolls, the father mumbled. The teacher did not seem particularly disturbed over this, and the family went away reassured that Walter would get over it.

The family undoubtedly would have forgotten the matter entirely had not the father just then discovered the dolls which he had locked away were missing. A search by the family uncovered them in Walter's closet, deep in the back, lined up in a careful row. The father decided this had now definitely become a problem. Something had to be done about it. When, a few days later, the mother found Walter in his room cutting up her best red frock for doll clothes, the family agreed something had to be done right away.

Walter was sent to military school. They will teach him to put away childish things, the father said. Walter's difficulty with military life became apparent almost at once, and the commandant began to question Walter's fitness for a military career. He participated barely at all in the athletic program and was the constant object of prank and complaint from the other cadets. The issue was settled when, during a routine inspection, an unusually large doll was found ill-concealed beneath the blanket of Walter's bunk. Walter was discharged before the end of the year with a letter from the commandant to the family expressing the belief that Walter's development as a boy was perhaps not entirely normal.

The family decided Walter had to be psychoanalyzed. A local doctor was retained to examine him. After what to the father seemed a suspiciously large number of trips to the doctor's office, the doctor announced his findings to the family. There's nothing wrong with Walter, the doctor said. He is probably artistic and ought not be expected to enjoy rifles or insensitive people. The doctor declared that, in his estimation, he did not believe, furthermore, that there was anything lacking in the parents, the family environment, the childhood feeding, or the sexual identity of the boy. Only be careful you do not impede his development, he warned. He asked for a fee that aged the father by several years.

Walter was sent to a school for fine arts where he was left alone to develop his talent. He spent most of his time working on projects of his own choosing. When at the end of the year, the family came to observe his progress, they found that he had made and dressed twenty-five rather large dolls.

They had to agree with Walter's instructor that they were indeed artfully made. After the instructor explained that in many countries doll making was an art of considerable social acceptance, the family decided, with only a frown from the father, that Walter might well be left there. The only difficulty with Walter's dolls, the instructor said, is their size. They're a little too large. But he'll develop here.

Walter stayed on at the school and worked on his dolls. Each year the family came to see Walter, and each year the instructor praised the boy's work and spoke of the genuine artistry of his little people. The only trouble, he explained, is that they are much too big. They're getting bigger, grumbled the father. Yes they are, the instructor said. The father threatened to take the boy to another art school. You may certainly do so, the director said in a frank talk with the family. But, he continued, not another school would consider his admission in view of his special interests. Your son is highly advanced as a dollmaker, the director went on, but frankly behind in other subjects. The family urged the director to correct this imbalance and left, admonishing Walter to pay more attention to geometry and French. And people, the father added.

Unfortunately, when it came time for Walter normally to be graduated, the director had to refuse Walter his diploma. A very talented dollmaker, the director agreed, but not up to standards in his other subjects. I regret we cannot confer the diploma of this institution upon your son.

The family came to take Walter home. They learned that in all he had one hundred and forty-seven dolls, all of them extremely large. They found not a single school book. We've been duped, the father said angrily. He informed his son that his dollmaking career was at an end. Who would want a doll that big, he asked, holding up one of Walter's creations. It was very large. When the father announced that, furthermore, the dolls were to remain behind, Walter suddenly fell very ill. He did not recover until the director persuaded the father to rent the school truck to haul Walter's dolls home. No one came to say good-bye as the family drove off. We've been made fools of, the father muttered. Walter said nothing. He was gazing at the rather large doll seated next to him.

Walter was happy to be back in his room. His sister was married now so that he was able to place his dolls, those that his room would not accommodate, in her room. Walter went on making more dolls. The father complained at the dinner table that it was not right. Any proper son of his should be out earning a living. He tried to secure a position for Walter at his own company, but it turned out that Walter could not write the company's name or add a simple column of figures. His father's dinner conversation soon turned to other things and the matter was forgotten.

Trouble flared up momentarily when the father found six of Walter's dolls in the master bedroom. I won't have it, he shouted. I need the room, said Walter. Then it was decided by the family that something had to be done about Walter's dolls. That Christmas the friends of the family each received a doll from Walter with a little note written by the sister explaining, in almost the exact words the family had heard them, the high art of dollmaking. Everyone made a big fuss over Walter's present since the dolls were really very lifelike and were indeed finely made. But an element of mirth was soon detected by the family in the reaction of the friends. After all, the family was finally told, they are rather large. Much too large for the children. The doll Walter gave my Junior, one mother said, is bigger than he is, and Junior is a normal five year old. Besides, she announced, Junior doesn't play with dolls.

Seedings

The family withdrew after that, unable to see any solution, but relieved that they had at least significantly reduced the number of Walter's little people. Little giants, the father grumbled. Things went along fairly peacefully until one evening at dinner, the father looked up from his plate and saw in the chair next to Walter, once occupied by the sister, a doll large enough to have her hands on the table. That's the limit, the father cried. The dolls had to go.

Walter unexpectedly got a job just then. The sister, though married, had not been inactive on the family's behalf. She arranged a position for Walter with one of the local department stores. Walter was to make mannequins. The father was very suspicious when Walter took over the entire basement and part of the garage for his work. But when Walter received his first pay check and the father saw that it was larger than his own, he kept silent. The mother and the sister dragged out Walter's dolls, especially the earlier, smaller ones, to show anyone who came to the house. There were frequent drives downtown to the department store to show friends Walter's art work in the store windows. Much nicer than the other mannequins, they said of Walter's dolls. They look so real, someone commented.

Walter soon made enough mannequins to satisfy every imaginable need the department store might have. Additional mannequins were stored in the basement to more than meet demand for years to come. Thank you, we have enough now, the department store manager told Walter. His salary was stopped and a short while later a number of mannequins were returned with an explanation that they were in excess of requirements.

The Man I Called Father

Walter went without work after that and the family waters again were becoming troubled. It's getting too crowded in here, the father complained. Walter's dolls were now lining the walls of every room of the house. Just when the strain on the family was nearing the dangerous point, Walter was invited by a marionette company to construct its puppets. When the family realized that Walter would be traveling with the company, they could scarcely conceal their pleasure.

Walter left in a whirl of family excitement and best wishes. Walter is a true artist, the family announced to the friends. The family readily agreed that soon as Walter got settled, they would ship, at the family's own expense, all his dolls to him. We, of course, will want to keep one or two of them for ourselves. One of the earlier, smaller dolls, they agreed. One week after Walter left to join the company they shipped all his dolls off.

They avidly awaited news of Walter's success. There was some small reference to a marionette company that some friend had read about in an out-of-town newspaper. That must be Walter, they said, nearly in tears over his success.

There was nothing more after that. As the months passed, the family began to speak less and less of Walter. One evening at the dinner table, the sister, her own growing son now occupying the seat Walter once had, asked in a loud voice, where is Walter. The parents did not know. We must find Walter, the sister said. Yes, the mother said, trying to think of the name of the company he was with. I can't get away right now, the father said. The months passed. The mother and the sister began to worry. Why doesn't he write, the mother asked. He can't write, the father replied. Why don't we write, the sister said. Finally the mother remembered the name of Walter's marionette company, and a letter was composed and sent off, asking about Walter.

Three weeks later, a reply came all the way from California. Walter was no longer with the company, the letter explained very courteously. There was no doubt about Walter's ability, but a difficulty had unfortunately arisen right from the start over the question of the size of the puppet dolls. Walter made them much too large, the letter complained, and had to be let go. His exact whereabouts was not known, but, the letter went on, he may have settled in the city where the relations were severed. That's the city we sent Walter's dolls to, the sister said.

This is getting serious, the mother said. Yes, the sister agreed, we must find Walter. He may need us. The family set out within a few weeks, as soon as the father was able to get away. They checked all the hotels and better class men's residences. They checked the art agencies, better department stores and some theaters. Let us try a notice in the newspaper, the sister said. They placed a notice asking for information about an artist specializing in the making of dolls for artistic purposes. Then they settled in their hotel and waited.

A week later an unsigned letter arrived, stating that a person loosely answering that description was known to have lived at such and such an address.

The family found that the address took them into the worst part of town to a building that appeared completely deserted and obviously about to be torn down. There was no sign of life anywhere. Most of the windows were boarded up. The near-by buildings were also empty and in various stages of demolition.

We're too late, the father said. Let's go inside, the sister said. Nobody could be living here, the mother said. They tried a room on the first floor whose door was ajar. The room was empty except for rubble and trash left behind by some former tenant. Let's try the others, the sister said. They were empty and deserted. The second floor, the sister said. There are four floors, the father said. We could call, the mother said. Walter, she cried aloud, as she used to do when he was a very small boy. There was no answer. We're too late, the father said. The second floor, the sister insisted. The second floor was as the first. Doors stood half ajar, revealing empty rooms. The third floor, the sister said. He's clearly not living here any more, the father said, poking his head into a doorway. There is a room we have not checked, the sister said, at the end of the hall. They went into it and stopped. Among the rubble in the far corner of the room lay an immense arm. This was Walter's room, the mother said after a silence. We're too late, the father said. The fourth floor, the sister said.

They pushed open the first door on the fourth floor. Empty, the father said. The others, the sister said. They worked their way down the hall. Empty, the father repeated. Look, the sister said, standing in a doorway, pointing. A huge foot lay in the middle of the bare floor, a stocking clung to it, unfulfilled. How gruesome, said the mother. It's indecent, said the father. There's one more door, said the sister.

They stood before it. You open it, the sister said to the mother. Oh, no, you open it, the mother said to the father. What nonsense, the father said throwing the door wide open. A silent mass, an incredible throng of gigantic dolls stared down and out at them. Amazons, the father cried stepping back. The place is solid with them. There was no way into the room but by removing the giant dolls. We must find Walter, the sister said, her arms lifting a doll half again as big as she out into the hall. The father tried pushing. The dolls would not yield. Do as I do, the sister said, lifting a second doll about the thighs. They slowly pried their way into the room and filled the hallway. There is a bed here, the sister said. I can't see, the mother said, trying to peer over the shoulders of the dolls looming before her. There's something in the bed, the sister said. Nothing but dolls, the father grumbled, lifting an amazon away to see.

They all saw at once. In the bed lay an utterly naked eight-foot doll of unbelievable beauty. In the bed beside her, also naked, lay Walter, clutching her in hungry, week-long death.

5

If the reader has read the foregoing with any discernment, certain things must have become fairly obvious about my psychological and moral state at the time of this first encounter with Doc. Delicacy forbids me from elaborating in very much detail, but it must be acknowledged here (as you may have gathered by now) that I had an unresolved problem with what can be technically called my libido. Put simply, I did not know what to do with the affective part of my nature. My marriage would have normally been expected to take care of such matters but this was not a successful marriage from many points of view. Put as bluntly as possible, my affective life was like a whale and I was like

Jonah trapped in its belly. I had little control over where this whale took me. I would cry out and all I heard was the echo of my own distress, leaving me with a feeling of hopelessness oftentimes bordering on despair. Only later would I realize how very much these cries were indeed being heard, and indeed, how God's ears are attuned to such cries, and very particularly to cries born of a disordered affective life. In a real sense the story that I am relating in this book is the tale of my release from the belly of that whale.

I beg my reader to bear with me if I delve somewhat into these waters. Each malady has its own medicine; only in knowing something of the sickness can the aptness of the remedy be seen. I hasten to add that it is not just my problem I describe here, but a problem of our time, if not a problem for all time. I tell my story freely and gladly, for whatever hesitation I might feel is quickly overcome by wonder and gratitude, and the hope that its telling might mean something to others.

I was born with a nature that must have needed affection and attention (including correction) beyond what it got in its early years. Normally the emotional needs of a child are satisfied by the attentions of healthy parents and the give-and-take of siblings. As the above story about Walter might suggest, this was not the case in my own childhood. It was not that my parents were cold, or that the sibling relationships were stressful. What was missing was a functional father, a father attentive enough to keep this particular son of his and his needs in focus, a father attentive enough to know when his son needed a father's sometimes firm, sometimes loving hand. I had a father who provided well for his family, materially speaking, but he never became engrossed in his children, never took a real interest in us. Speaking for myself, my father and I were like good neighbors of casual acquaintance waving at each other from our separate driveways — eager to keep on good terms but having little if anything to do with each other. Like a casual neighbor, my father knew some general things about me, but that was about it as far as I could ever tell. I never once in those growing-up years had a heart-to-heart talk with him, never once poured myself out to him, or felt he had revealed something of himself to me. Never once did I receive a token from my father indicating he had caught on to some secret inclination of my nature. I never saw my father study me; if he did, he did not seem to understand or perhaps even like what he saw. I never recall ever feeling his approval, but still carry with me the memory of his irritation with me, and sometimes, as in Walter's case, his outright disapproval. In the end I turned away from my father and turned inwards, much as Walter did. In the end I took on the privileges and responsibilities of being my own father. It was all done covertly. In my conscious processes, I honored and rather liked my father. I was always proud of him when he received promotions at the bank, and sad for him at professional setbacks. I admired him because he had had to overcome so much in his own fatherless childhood, and he was by any measure a successful, respectable person. But at heart I became a secret rebel, privately convinced that this exceptionally good man, my father, could do *me* little good.

I have since come to understand that there are things that a son must learn about himself that can only be learned through a father, or someone functioning as a father. One of those things is the special thrill of cooperative work, experienced when a young son is invited to work alongside his father on some project and then at some point is allowed to grab hold and do some operation by himself. The boy fumbles a bit and his father reaches to steady his hand or correct an angle, and for a moment it looks like it might end in disaster. But then suddenly the work falls into place and the boy hears his father utter those magic words, "Nice going, son." The pleasure such praise arouses in a boy cannot be overstated. But more important than that, a boy's introduction into cooperative work with his father, and the experience of being trusted with a piece of that work and of being able to accomplish it, all to the music of his father's praise, takes the boy out of himself and of that world his mother had nurtured him in since birth. A new appetite is being aroused, moving the boy to leave that world and trail after his father, hungry for more of this male affirmation. And to the extent that the father stoops to satisfy this need in his son, the child quite naturally becomes his. A mature and healthy father is thus able to guide his son into experiences of the objective world, and open him up to the satisfactions of addressing that world, of confronting its problems and solving them, however minute the scale initially. And he corrects his son too, in a way that enables the son to accept it, teaching him the need to conform to a reality outside himself, to find the right angle, apply just the right pressure, use the correct tool, face a mistake like a man and re-do the operation until it is right, and so on. In the process, the son absorbs his father's values and way of seeing things, of walking and talking, and more importantly the boy absorbs his father's self-confidence, his patience and objectivity, and learns through all this the ego-pleasure of standing on his own two feet and coping. In short he discovers the pleasures and discipline of being a man. It is not something a mother can accomplish for her son, or a wife for her husband. Thus from the hands of a father, or an older man functioning as a father, the son experiences desires and satisfactions of a kind he otherwise would not suspect existed. Without a functioning father, unaware of the manly satisfactions that await his struggle with an objective order, the boy will seek gratification elsewhere, in imagination and in extensions of that easy, intimate, accepting world where the mother's love was originally felt and cherished. In the process, the son withdraws from his father, assuaging the guilt with bitter reflections about the old man's indifference, just as I have done here. The boys grows up a rebel, secret or overt, and the father of such a rebel becomes at worst a roadblock to be knocked aside, and at best an irrelevance, like an out-of-season window piece that no one pays attention to.

Very early in life this became my story. I had the natural longing of any boy for a relationship with his father; I used to look for him but he was not there for me, not in a way that really mattered. My father was hardly to blame; his own childhood had been both fatherless and motherless, and his upbringing was far and away more deprived than mine. But whatever the cause, I came to look to my mother and eventually to women in general for the emotional gratification I needed. They were available to me; my father was not. I came to believe that whatever it was I needed would come only from women's hands. How could my father help me in this? For that matter, how could any woman help, since I would place on her expectations no woman could satisfy. Thus enters the need for woman in all her facets, for many women, a sealed room filled to overflowing with a plenitude of women, all larger than life, and all unable in the end to make up for a father and the ineffable thrill a father confers when he tells the boy at his side, "Good work, son."

One can hear St. Joseph saying the same words to Jesus as the boy stood at his side in the family workshop and lent his small hands to some task. And is not this the same affirmation the mature Jesus received from his heavenly Father that time at the river Jordan? *This is my beloved Son in whom I am well pleased.* What sort of life does a man have when this affirmation was missing in his formative years? What restless lifelong hunger does its absence give rise to?

6

Spoke to my director and he is convinced I should go back to New York, sometime in May. I am still dizzy after all that happened in New York. (From a letter of Doc's to Howie's girlfriend, Cindy, dated April 5th, 1960.)

Doc returned to New York two weeks later, and this time he stayed with us as a houseguest for over a month, sleeping on the couch in our living room like a member of the family, though in reality he was far too imposing a presence to be family. It was more like having a lion sleeping in your living room, but a lion you found you could have fun with, even if you were always a little cautious with him. Doc quickly became the center of our day and indeed of our life and for a month we were almost inseparable. Nor was it any hardship, once you gave in to the notion that he had taken over your life. It was only to be for a little while and besides, being with him like that always left you feeling elated and privileged. But those days took on the character of a crucible too. Doc was too discerning and I had too much to hide for me not to feel heat in his presence, even if the heat were nothing more than the kindest form of attention. To say the least, sustained attention like that was something new and unsettling for someone like me. I hadn't had it as a boy; I couldn't cope with it naturally as a man.

For all that, the time passed quickly. There were lots of parties, lots of forays out into the Village, lots of superb music, lots of mind-stretching discussions, lots and lots of laughter. Something interesting, indeed captivating, was always going on, often with a small band of my Village friends who were similarly attracted. We ate well and often, and once Doc even took us to an ice-cream parlor, in the company of friends who could easily have been smoking pot the night before. We all ate our treats with gusto. It made us feel innocent and clean to be with him, as if we were children again. But something else was happening too, to me at least, something big, far too big for my mind to get its thoughts around. And then one day I woke up and realized that life for me was never going to be the same again: not in what I believed about God, about myself, about the church I worked for, about what I would do for a living, what I wanted for my life. My life as I knew it had run out of room indeed. Or to put it another way, I woke up one day and saw that someone had moved in on me. I was no longer a solitary man. I could no longer hide even if I wanted to. I was in the process of acquiring a father.

* * *

There was a truly huge, colorful, abstract expressionist oil painting that dominated the far wall of our living room where Doc slept; it had to be the first thing to catch your eye on entering. The painting was done by a Japanese abstract expressionist, Taro Yamamoto, another acquaintance of mine. I wasn't crazy about the picture: it looked like an aerial map of the midwest, with each state a different rectangle of color (e.g. dull orange, deep blue-black, etc.), against which background was pitted a huge bold splash of color, applied thickly like some outer space eruption across the region. Something in the painting caught your attention for a minute or two and then you tended to ignore it. Taro was a serious enough painter; his work was being handled by an uptown gallery and some of his paintings had recently been picked up by the Huntington, an uptown private art museum owned by a wealthy New Englander of that name who sponsored promising talent. I got the painting from Taro for a song, for less actually than his costs in canvas and paints. Basically it covered a huge wall in our apartment that needed covering. Looking back, the painting probably had something remotely erotic about it. This may have been what led Doc to do something rather unthinkable for a houseguest under normal social circumstances.

Seedings

I don't think he had been back with us more than a few days when Doc went up to Taro's painting with a piece of charcoal and began printing some letters on a large patch of white. It was Latin: *Negra sed pulchra sum. Do you know what it means?* Doc asked. I was a little stunned, and since my Latin at that time was practically non-existent, he translated, *I am black but beautiful,* explaining that the words were uttered by the Mother of God. I am not sure when or where she said them, or what the words signify actually, and I don't know why he wrote them on our painting. At the time I found it rather annoying. It was a strange way of introducing us to the Blessed Mother, if that was his purpose. Probably it was his reaction to what he sensed about the painting.

Doc had a singular devotion to the Blessed Mother and one of the next things he did was to give Terry and me a large portrait of Our Lady of Guadalupe. That picture immediately took on special meaning for us, as it has continued to do to this day. I eventually came to understand a great deal about Mary and the role she plays in the redemption of souls, all learned existentially, I might add. I was about to enter a path behind this man that would lead into a furnace of truthfulness, and Mary would be there for me just as she was there for her son on the Way of the Cross, and just as she is for all who are called to carry a cross of truth. It is because of her and what we receive through her that sinners can say, in their own right, *I am black but beautiful.*

Actually it was the Mother of God who brought Doc to us, not the other way around – with some critical assistance from her spouse, St. Joseph. Let me tell you why I think this was the case. Some months before Doc came to us that first time, I was walking down 14th street late one morning, between 7th and 8th avenues. I had been visiting a painter in a nearby loft, a particularly attractive young woman who had asked me to come to her studio to look over her work. She was a talented artist and I was thinking of giving her a show at the art gallery I had just started. What I relate here happened immediately after I had spent an hour conversing with this artist about her paintings. As we talked, I had begun to feel myself being almost irresistibly drawn to her in a physical way, so much so in fact that I abruptly took my leave. I began walking home, down 14th street, not a little disturbed by the morning's experience. I found myself walking past the little Catholic church, Our Lady of Guadalupe, situated on the north side of the street. For some reason I stopped to look at the picture of Our Lady that in those days used to be on the building wall almost at eye-level right by the entrance. Of course I didn't know anything about Our Lady of Guadalupe; to me this was just some obscure Latin American icon. But I stopped before the picture, wondering about its strange beauty. I remember thinking that this image – and the Lady behind the image – belonged to a world I was completely shut out of, that she represented a spirituality I could never expect to know or understand. The thought made me suddenly sad for some reason, as if there was in me a desire that it might not be so. The feeling had nothing to do with unsatisfied curiosity; it was actually more like envy. But why someone in my Protestant shoes should react like that remains a mystery to me. Why feel sad and envious over the image of an

Indian woman, from a distant place that had nothing to do with me? I have always believed it was Mary who stopped me, that she had seen me passing by that morning and called out to me, or more likely simply reached out and took me by the ear. It's in my nature to always want the best for myself, and it was to that appetite I guess that Mary appealed. It's probably true then that this interior step toward the Catholic Church was motivated by envy over a beauty and a good I felt shut off from. But Mary's reasons for grabbing me that morning had to do with something else, with another part of my nature that would soon get me into troubled waters, and for which I needed her help.

Around that time I had become involved with a woman member of the Protestant church I was serving. She was a lonely woman, not especially attractive, not even particularly bright, but intelligent enough and friendly and not without charm; and she liked to talk about God. Moreover, she had taken a strong liking to me. She was active in the church and through the not infrequent gatherings that typified this church, we got to know each other quite well. On the surface she seemed normally happy, but in reality she had a load of psychological problems, mostly having to do with her mother, and was undergoing therapy. But she could laugh at herself too, and anyway it seemed almost every third person those days was in therapy or talking about it. But then one day she lost her job clerking for a religious bookstore, and she seemed to go into a tailspin after that. After a number of months it became apparent that she was making no effort to look for another work, and those of us who cared about her became concerned. She lived alone in an apartment just a few blocks from the church, and now rarely went out except perhaps to attend some church affair. This went on for almost a year and by now it was clear she was becoming dysfunctional. I began to call on her mornings, since she lived so close by the church, to urge her to get out to seek work somewhere, all without much success. Then gradually I found myself lingering during those visits. We would have coffee and long talks and it all became rather cozy. Then one morning on my way to her apartment I felt the full force of the impurity that had begun to operate inside these little visits. Only the night before I had dropped by to chat with her. It was late but she was in a lively mood and wanted to go out and have some fun. Her idea was to go down to Battery Park and take a ride on the Staten Island ferry which was about the last thing in the world I wanted to do at that hour. But maybe she'd like to see the new Ray Gun exhibit at the gallery. I would open the Gallery up and there was this painting by Jim Dine that you entered. Mercifully, she wasn't interested and the night soon petered out.

But impurity leered at me barefaced the next morning and I realized I had to put an end to these house calls. Only I found I couldn't. I found myself instead heading to her apartment, literally unable to re-direct my steps. On the way, out of desperation, I slipped inside a Catholic Church a block from her place (Corpus Christi). I had never been inside this church before but I immediately went up to a statue of St. Joseph, knelt down, and began to beg him for help. St. Joseph had never meant anything at all to me in the past, but I must say I sought the help of this saint now, long and hard. I must have stayed there half an hour, maybe longer, and then I left. I saw this woman that morning all the same – I still had no control over the matter – but the mood had changed and the morning passed uneventfully after all. The pull of this set-up, though – an inviting, lonely young woman who always brightened at my visit, and my own unfulfilling marriage – would not go away, and the situation would get more complicated over the next few weeks before it got better; indeed before it took a sudden, unexpected turn, an early consequence of a telephone call from my friend Howie announcing that his friend Doc was in town.

Let me say something here about Joseph, the Worker, the saint who raised Jesus from boyhood to manhood, the saint I had called upon for help so desperately that morning. One day, maybe 18 months following this episode at Corpus Christi church – after my little family and I had become Catholic and left the Village scene to live with Doc in a little village just outside the city – he and I were huddled together late one night building something with a Meccano construction set. In those days Doc and I used to spend hours (the one leading, the other struggling to conform and cooperate) constructing such things as trucks and cranes, all with motors and elaborate gear trains and the like. The essence of the work was that everything had to be done peacefully and with complete recollection, like two monks at work whose slow, deliberate, harmonious movements made their work a form of prayer. Such play was always a spiritual work for Doc; one could not be with him in such circumstances without praying in one's heart, lest a separation take place between us like that between oil and water. But prayer as such was more a matter of disposition and interior orientation than actual words: even pious thoughts would have been a distraction and when working with this man there could be no distraction if things were to go smoothly. You worked as if in the presence of a great king, a king who expected you to focus on what you were doing, not on him or anything else. But you weren't ever to forget whose presence you were in, or for whose sake you were doing the work. That king was God, you understand, not Doc, but Doc was there as attendant of that king to let you know, sometimes by just a glance, when your attention began to stray (usually to sink back into your own thoughts) or, conversely, when the success of some operation began to mean too much. He called it working in a state of recollection. One can imagine Joseph working with the boy Jesus in his carpentry shop in just this manner. Of course, Jesus would have taken to it by nature. For myself, it was a great struggle at first. I gradually learned what this recollection thing was all about by pure induction, by floundering and being corrected time and time again until recollection became a habit, a second nature. But, as I started to say, one night as we were working together in this quiet, peaceful, ultimately satisfying way, I recall Doc suddenly looking up at me and saying, *You know, Paul, I have the feeling St. Joseph has an awful lot to do with what we're doing here right now.*

7

During that month Doc stayed with us in the Village, it was his wit perhaps more than anything that eventually disarmed the reservations of this rebel. It seemed he always reached Terry through music, but for me, at least initially, it was this incredible wit that convinced me God was behind this man. His wit generally left me in awe. But it wasn't cleverness as such or the incredible intelligence showing through that struck me so much as its aptness to the occasion, and the way that wit was used, never to humiliate its object or to celebrate its author. To the contrary, there was always something spiritually pedagogical motivating the wit and it was this providential benefit that convinced me God was behind him.

It was Doc's *puns* especially that struck me as almost preternatural, as if God had set up things in language just so that this man could make some play on words, a play so exquisitely *a propos* of the moment as to make me marvel, time and again. The situations with their punctuating puns exploded like little firecrackers all through the day, each catching you unawares and causing you to wonder at its apposition to something going on in your mind just then. Unlike most puns, these made you see, not wince. They had the effect of illuminating and redirecting the way you thought about things. Unfortunately I remember only the barest handful of them, which I repeat here with apologies since they lack their context and as a result much of their impact.

We were speaking of modern poetry one evening, something I was generally taken with, when Doc volunteered his summary of the modern situation: *The history of modern poetry, or from bard to verse.* This was followed up by a little poetic offering of his own, in the spirit of the times: *Don't know why I metaphor, metafornication.* While we were discussing epistemology one day, a favorite topic of mine, he mused that epistemology sounded to him a lot like *It appears to me, O Gee.* And once, talking about modern Biblical criticism, he said that *exegesis* should be spelled *exit Jesus.* Puns like these flowed out of him in a torrent in those weeks he was with us. One day we heard the Simon and Garfunkel song *Scarborough Fair* over the radio with its refrain *Parsley, Sage, Rosemary and Thyme.* Doc took it all in for a moment and then cracked, *Partly sage, Rosemary needs time.* And so on, endlessly, to everyone's great delight but perhaps most especially to mine.

This was the honeymoon stage. Later his humor became more surgical. For example, once, some years later when we were living in a small house just outside the city, Doc had been away for a few hours and when he returned to his room he found me busily waxing the floor. I must have looked at him a little expectantly, hoping for some expression of approval since it was *his* room I was waxing after all. Instead he said, *I see you are waxing. Would that you were waning.* Doc was simply using the pun to teach me something, like the dictum of St. John the Baptist, *He must increase and I must decrease,* applying it to me at a moment when I was waxing with a sense of my own virtue. As you can see, by this time he was like an abbot to those of us around him, a superior whose humor at times was no longer so funny, so easy to take.

I had yet to learn that self-directed humor was a precious gift of faith, a merciful salve for the troubled conscience, but that's because I was the quintessential *goy* who found laughing at himself an unnatural act. It's rather mysterious how Jews laugh at themselves. It seems they are the only people who make themselves the butt of their own humor. Doc used to say that the difference between the Jew and the gentile was that the Jew knew he wasn't God; the gentile wasn't so sure. And of course you don't laugh at God.

Doc knew how to laugh with the laughter of faith. He made us laugh a lot, and somehow the laughter always brought us closer to God. Humor was his antidote to the deep-seated misgiving we have about ourselves, a misgiving that keeps most of us doubting that God could love us. He used humor to reassure us we can always go to God, no matter what. Humor was Doc's way of correcting false notions about how we as creatures must relate to the Creator, his way of puncturing our futile attempts to base that relationship on our own goodness. Humor was his way of letting the creature *be* creature, his way of putting our shortcomings in their place, for in light of God's redemptive act in Jesus, none of these shortcomings need keep us from Him. Humor was Doc's way of loosening the stranglehold that the accursed Accuser exercises over our consciences, creating false consciences in us. Humor was Doc's way of liberating those destined to become saints. At least that's how the process began, and it will end that way too. *The wise shall laugh in the latter day (Prov. 31:25).*

Probably nothing could convey the pedagogical thrust of his wit better than the limericks he liked to compose, and at one time in his life he composed them in abundance. They, perhaps more than anything, convey the character and motive of his wit — a rare combination of charity and brutal candor that turns the ordinary limerick into occasions of fraternal correction, an instruction that could lead, to those so inclined, to the rarest of gifts — self-knowledge.

It is not hard to envision the particular subject who inspired each of these poems, typically sitting across from Doc at a table in some coffee shop, when suddenly, as he was wont to do, he would take out a piece of paper and with a merry grin begin his little operation on the by-this-time suspecting soul. His limericks invariably have that rapier's tip to them, but the intent is never to harm but to help, with self-knowledge. That he was even moved to do this was unusual, that he could do this with such artful humor is simply unique.

> This is a poem about a girl
> Who tried to be a saint,
> And worried night and day for fear
> Of what she thought her taint.
> Oh would that she might learn at last
> How just to make her humble
> The suavity of God devised
> That taint to let her stumble.

> There was a young sister who said:
> "I wonder if I am misled,
>   I give the dear Lord
>   All the merits I've stored,
> And He keeps on shaking His head."

> There once was a delicate lass
> Who couldn't abide anything crass,
>   Said she: "If I can't

Seedings

>Have Gregorian chant
I'll just stay away from Mass."

This is a poem about Miss Apprehension
Who led a life of constant tension
>Sometimes she'd reason
>And sometimes she'd balk
But whatever she did took the form of talk.

There is a certain woman
Who isn't very certain,
For every time you look at her
She quickly draws the curtain.

I think his meekness is a sign,
That all that's meek is not divine.

I know a woman who is sly,
I wish that she were slyer;
For then perhaps she would confess
That she's an awful liar.

This is a poem about a girl named Rose
Who got herself deeper and deeper in woes,
Nothing she did seemed to be any use,
It got so bad it became an excuse.
She had in its plenitude the gift of tears,
They flowed from her eyes, from her nose, from
>her ears.
And no one suspected her depths of self-pity,
'Til one day a flood destroyed the whole city.
And then not a soul was left to surmise

The Man I Called Father

The power behind Rose's innocent eyes,
Including poor Rose, who at last found her
  rest,
Or maybe she didn't, but let's hope for the
  best.

There was a young fellow named Jack
Who went round on a circular track.
    Said he in despair,
    "I'm getting nowhere,"
So he turned around and went back.

There was a young lady named Alice,
Who said, "I must drink of my chalice.
    O, how lovely is pain,
    In the form of champagne,
Let others consider their malice."

He wrote these sorts of things about himself as well, fully able to laugh at himself like any good Jew.

    This philosophical guy called Doc
    Is a most disagreeable man.
    His friends (though they won't admit it)
    Avoid him when they can.
    If only they'd admit it —
    But, then, he won't permit it!

I once witnessed the composition of a limerick of his, one which was rather remarkable in my opinion. It was a late Sunday afternoon. There were six or eight of us sitting around chatting with him. We had been talking at

Seedings

length about Jean Paul Sartre and had been having an interesting discussion when, suddenly, Doc closed his eyes and seemed to go far away. He stayed like that while the rest of us continued to chat and joke, but with one eye on what he was up to. It wasn't like he was lost in deep, deep thought. He actually seemed to be away on another planet, as though his body were still with us but he himself wasn't — almost as if the rest of us were at a wake, albeit a rather cheerful one. Anyway, after about ten minutes or so he came to and smiled. Without explanation, he asked for a piece of paper and wrote down verbatim the lines that I reproduce below.

>An elegant playboy named Sartre
>Said, "Pray, what's the use of a pater?
>>It's true that you need one
>>If only to seed one,
>But I'd rather have a self-starter."

That he should see Sartre and his existentialism entirely in light of Sartre's relationship (lack of one) with his father was quintessential Doc. As far as he was concerned, nothing shaped the development of an individual, great or small, so much as that individual's relationship to his father, or the other side of that coin, the father's relationship to the son. Truly, he saw everyone in this light.

>There was a young man named Freud,
>Whose spiritual life was destroyed
>>By the thought of a father
>>Who didn't even bother
>To let himself be annoyed.

8

At some point during the month that Doc was with us, we started going to the nine o'clock Mass at Our Lady of Guadalupe on 14th Street. These experiences in the company of a man who seemed so completely lost in what was transpiring on the altar were a very telling time for me. I had sometimes attended Catholic Mass years earlier while in the Air Force, but I had always been alone at such times, usually in a strange city, and as a Protestant I never became very involved in what was going on in the sanctuaries of these churches; what had attracted me then were the long peaceful silences and the feeling – hardly understood – of something sacred taking place, but that was all. Attending Mass in the company of this man and participating in the liturgy through him turned the Latin Mass into an utterly new, undreamed of experience. I would hear his breathing turn to silence as he became more lost in prayer, trying to pray that way myself. Holding a shared missal, my eyes would follow his over the Latin prayers, sensing what the words meant to him. Kneeling beside him after his reception of the Host, I would become aware of how long and deep his breathing now became, wishing I too could have received Jesus but taking comfort knowing that Doc had promised to receive the Body of Christ for me. This time it was more than the aesthetics of the scene that mattered, though truthfully the things in this little church that struck my senses and aroused such feelings became a most important part of what led me to the Catholic faith.

At the conclusion of Mass, we would linger in our seats to pray – Doc, his eyes closed, his head slightly bowed, seemed alert to some internal goings on after Mass and indeed would sometimes jot things down. And then we would go and make a leisurely visit to various of the statues of the saints and of Our Lady. He clearly felt at home in this church and moved about with a kind of filial familiarity. I was still the Protestant outsider but I quickly disliked being an outsider in this place; some appetite far down in my own nature was aroused and I wanted to feel I too belonged here. Without fail, just before we left, Doc would take our four-year-old daughter, Sarah, to the statue of St. Thérèse of Lisieux, popularly called The Little Flower, and they would kneel down together, cross themselves and say a special prayer. Then we would all go have a merry breakfast at a little luncheonette across the street, a practice which became very much a part of the morning ritual.

I was being introduced in the most privileged way conceivable to the mystery of mysteries – the Eucharist – by someone who loved and participated in this mystery with immense faith, buttressed by unparalleled intelligence and sensibility. But the reader should understand that it was not human agency that brought about the changes that were taking place in my life. Something had begun to transpire in my own heart of hearts during these moments in this little church – this little sanctuary of Our Lady, so different from anything I had ever known before – with its high vaulted ceiling, its walls darkened from years of candles burning through the night, dark windowless walls lined with statuary seemingly made supple through prayer, the wall above the altar illuminated by Our Lady's lovely deep blue image, and the beauty of the altar itself beneath her, marble white and appointed with gold, its gilded tabernacle doors now shut tight, the semi-dark ambiance that settled in when lights were turned down after Mass, the peaceful ever-flicker of candles, the presence of individuals scattered here and there in the darkened pews reluctant to leave, some handling rosary beads, others just seeming to imbibe the peace of this holy space, we among them, all because of what had just transpired on the altar. This holy place intoxicated my starved and dried-up soul and left me powerless before its appeal, which is just as it should be and was meant to be.

My mind and my affective life for the first time in thirty-one years were finding something they could actually get together on. That, I tell you, is no small thing; for me it was the beginning of a whole life. If you have ever been pulled apart as I was, emotions pursuing things the mind could never justify, and the mind in its turn pursuing things that left the feelings cold, if your affective life has ever wandered off like an alley cat, leaping from one trashcan to another, looking for what it might find in this book, this bar, this face, this city, this world, while the mind was busy elsewhere taking pains not to notice, then you will understand me. I was being healed by the grace of God and the intercession of Our Lady. It would take years and many trials before this all ran its course, but the seedling the sower had so recently planted was sinking its tendrils into rich black earth and would survive. In the mystery of sacred liturgy I found something I could embrace the way a man embraces a woman, and yet stand in awe of with all the powers of my mind. There were times when the joy of this was almost more than I could bear, as when the priest-monks of this blessed chapel would be gathered in the recess of their choir loft, voices blending in plainsong that wafted over us like a gentle breeze, communicants silently filing to the altar rail to kneel and receive the great gift of Christ's Body, and this alley cat, rescued who knows why, feeling the stir of wholesome life spreading out its roots.

I remember a distinguished professor of mine at Union Theological Seminary in Manhattan once describing the scene of a typical Catholic church on any given Sunday. (This was in the days of the Latin Mass.) The edifice, he said, would be bulging with standing room only, people literally spilling out onto the sidewalk, a phenomenon to be repeated every hour from early Sunday morning until noon. Police would be outside unsnarling traffic as activity in the surrounding streets periodically came to a standstill, as if some major event were taking place inside this building. Do you know why this phenomenon is repeated Sunday after Sunday in these churches, the professor asked? By this time of course we were all mentally contrasting the scene he drew with the orderly 11 o'clock Protestant service most of us were familiar with, where everyone is assured of a seat with room to spare. The professor answered his question with a hint of envy in his voice. It was, he explained, because *God is present in the tabernacles of these churches!* And so He is. I do not know if that Protestant theologian really believed what he said to his class that day; I know that by this time I was beginning to believe it, with everything I had.

The unanswered question was what was I going to do about it? I sensed that Terry had already made her decision about the Catholic Church, so it came down to what I would do. Despite all that I said above about my great attraction to the liturgy, I still had hesitations, not unlike my ambiguous reaction towards Doc the first time I met him, only now the shadow that loomed across my path was much, much larger. The Catholic Church represented authority, and entering this Church meant having to obey it. Nothing in my thirty-one years had prepared me for obedience. I had learned to slip out from under parental authority whenever it suited me ever since my early teens; was I to return to authority now and one so pervasive? And there was this other thing: the Church's Magisterium was deeply interested in my soul, well and good, but it would not be the least bit interested in my mind, except of course to form it. Yet the only life I knew, that mattered to me, was the life of the mind, the life of ideas. I had floods of original ideas, indeed I lived for them, and the thought of entering a world that would take no interest in them seemed like a form of mental suicide. I had met a few priests by this time and always found them nice and easy to relate to; they seemed more immediate, less abstract, less unsure deep down than their typical Protestant counterpart. But I had always to be on their wavelength; invariably the moment I would try to get them to be on mine the expression in their eyes turned cloudy. The Catholic mind, whether priest or laity, was not what you would call open; fresh, interesting ideas didn't traffic there freely. The Catholic mind knew where to find God and how to serve him, and the right employment of the mind directly flowed from that. Ideas weren't anything to get too excited about (St. Thomas referred to his as "straw"). Not so for me, not so. To me the only life worth living took place in the mind. I dreamt one day of having an idea that would even change how we saw God. Such things might seem to border on delusion, but it went with the times. (Other so-called "thinkers" just then were announcing insights like "God is dead"; at least I knew better than that.) Often I sat like a watchman into the long hours of the night, looking, waiting for the comet of a new idea to flash off in the mind. I was always known as a thinker from early on. I had gotten a professor or two at Seminary to pay attention to half-ideas of mine. Pieces of mine were being published here and there in minor places and often they invoked commentary – like a breath of fresh air," a Protestant church official told me once in a late night call. I even got visits from *Time* magazine over something I wrote for *Exodus*. A few here and there were beginning to take notice: had a new and original thinker arrived on the scene? But the Catholic Magisterium would never take heed, not by its very nature. To the Church my soul was of infinite worth; my mind infinitely less so and undoubtedly in need of reforming. It was for me to heed the Magisterium's mind, believe what it said, do what it said, and, yes, be forbidden what it said could not be done, believed, read, eaten, and so on. Then there would be much hope for me.

(Recall that this was in the "neo-scholastic" days before Vatican II, before the age of dissent and cafeteria religion ("maybe some of this; think I'll pass on that"); when fasting for Sunday Mass, even to a glass of water, began at midnight Saturday; when standing on line to tell your sins to a priest was a regular and necessary event; when eating meat on Friday was a serious lapse, and intentionally missing Sunday Mass was a grave sin; when many popular movies and books were on the index of forbidden things; when a scholar needed special permission to read at will in the library; in short, when being a practicing Catholic meant you lived your life differently than non-Catholics, that is to say, under obedience to the Magisterium of the Church. That Church and the sort of Catholic lifestyle that went with it, in most of these respects, are hardly recognizable today.)

Then there was this final and perhaps greatest misgiving of all. I was gravely tempted to think the Church would wall me off from human desire. If the desiring part of my nature up to that point in my life had not fared very well, it was nevertheless what kept me going. I feared now the Church would cut me off from myself, from these inner wellsprings and the dream of their eventual fulfillment. I have already explained that there was a fundamental unhappiness in my marriage, a lack of fulfillment for both of us, as if the marriage had been a mistake. We remained close and faithful to each other in point of fact, but speaking for myself, my emotional life was on the loose. I looked into the faces of women everywhere I went. I don't think it was physical desire exactly, though disorders of that sort were at work as well, but fundamentally I think it was a case of Adam longing for an Eve, a companion to contain and complement his life. Adam of course had a perfectly balanced and rectified nature and any Eve would have been lucky to have him (and vice versa). Mine was a mess and unlikely to make any Eve very happy, no more than I had made Terry happy. But it was the only nature I had, and one way or the other, I had to provide for its happiness. Which is why I hesitated at the doors of the Church. How would my footloose search for satisfaction in some unknown person fare in a Church that talked about "custody of the eyes" and, of course, of far graver prohibitions? Not very well, I feared. Would not consenting to this Magisterium mean having to give up endless ruminations about good and evil, whether to go here or there, see this person or that person, pursue this idea or that, and so on and so on? If I entered this Church, would not virtually everything I desired, thought, and did be subject to another's judgment, another's will, one more consequential than my own? It would be God's will, but God's will interpreted not by me in the supple pathways of my own mind, over a glass of good red wine or maybe a stinger, but by a Magisterium which has been calling things by their same name for 2000 years. And making great saints in the process. Yes indeed, but half the time what I wanted for myself were these self-canonizing fantasies I was so adept at weaving. The bottom line was that conversion meant I had to change. So I kept coming back to where I was when all this started, knowing I had to change, not believing I ever could, and half not wanting to in any case, fearing it meant abandoning any hope of ever finding myself in the color of some woman's eyes.

In the end, God made it so easy for me. It is not an accident of grammar, I think, that the Church is spoken of as *she*. I could not have let go of my life and its secret, unsatisfied need, poor Walter that I was, had not this new, incipient love of the liturgical Church also been of woman, in the deepest, most mysterious and purest sense of that reality. Surely God knew what He was about when He ordained it that men should all come to Him through a woman, a woman called Wisdom in the Old Covenant and Mary in the New. Through her Son. And I might add, through those people and those accidents of time and place that situate this woman and her Son across our path.

Does not Wisdom call,
and understanding raise her voice?
On the top of the heights along the road,
at the crossroads she takes her stand;
By the gates at the approaches of the city,
by the entryways she cries aloud:
"To you, O men, I call:
my appeal is to the children of men.
You simple ones, gain resource,
you fools, gain sense.

"The Lord begot me, the first born of his ways,
the forerunner of his prodigies of long ago;
From of old I was poured forth,
at the first, before the earth.
When there were no depths I was brought forth,
when there were no fountains or springs of water;
Before the mountains were settled into place,
before the hills, I was brought forth;
While as yet the earth and the fields were not made
nor the first clods of the world.

"When he established the heavens I was there,
when he marked out the vault over the face
of the deep;

Seedings

> *When he made firm the skies above,*
> > *when he fixed fast the foundations of the earth;*
>
> *When he set for the sea its limit,*
> > *so that the waters should not transgress his command;*
>
> *Then was I beside him as his craftsman,*
> > *and I was his delight day by day.*
>
> *Playing before him all the while,*
> > *playing on the surface of his earth;*
>
> *And I found delight in the sons of men.*
>
> *"So now, O children, listen to me;*
> > *instruction and wisdom do not reject!*
>
> *Happy the man who obeys me,*
> > *and happy those who keep my ways,*
>
> *Happy the man watching daily at my gates,*
> > *waiting at my doorposts;*
>
> *For he who finds me finds life,*
> > *and wins favor from the Lord;*
>
> *But he who misses me harms himself;*
> > *all who hate me love death."*
>
> —Proverbs 8:1-5, 12-36

Can you now understand why, kneeling beneath the miraculous image of Our Lady, in this sacred space, next to a spiritual father who has just received the Body of Christ, feeling what is going on inside him at that moment and knowing that he has received this Jesus for me too, the way a good father would do before the son is able on his own? Can you see how all this could make me let go, forget my misgivings, my sad hunger, and for the first time in my life begin to desire the Father in

Heaven and the good that I saw coming to me from his hands, to want to belong to Him and be conformed to Him and to the spiritual father that Our Lady had sent me out of the Father's Providence? In the liturgical worship of the Mass, in the company of one who was far, far ahead of me in his journey to God yet right there at my side, I began to believe in the promise of a life far more wonderful, more transcendent than anything self-love ever dreamed of on its own, a promise moreover that became more real with every passing day. I could not let this pass me by. In the existential calculus that went on in my heart and mind those days, I came to realize that in giving up the *me* I had made of myself I would be losing nothing of worth but would be gaining everything – the me God had intended in the first place and that would be held forever safe in His keeping, which is to say – in this life – *in his Church*. In the end the very things I feared were what drew me to her – the Church's authority and strength, her wisdom, her maternal instrumentality in that providence the Father has ordained for each of his children, including this one.

The day my life changed for good, I woke up in a fiercely stubborn mood and announcing flatly to Terry over breakfast: *I've never been so far from becoming a Catholic in my entire life as I am today.* Terry just said nothing, and of course Sarah was too young to understand much of what was going on. (Sarah had no problem with any of this. She told Doc that she and he were twins except that he was older. As for the Church and the liturgy, she took to it all as naturally as a duck takes to water.) Doc had stayed elsewhere the previous night and we were meeting him for lunch at Howard Johnson's on Eighth Street. Everyone showed up on the dot, all six of us regulars, hungry as usual. We got a table but instead of the usual good spirits that overtook us at such times, our party seemed flat and disjointed. The atmosphere got no better as the meal went on. Doc made some off-hand remarks about returning to Mexico in the next few days, news that clearly called for talk about the future, but none was forthcoming. I think it was at this point that I began to panic. I knew something extraordinary had been shown to me and I was about to see it slip away. But there was more to it than that. As I sat there, feeling more and more uncomfortable, I saw with utmost clarity that I could never go back to the life I had been leading before the advent of this man. There was nothing in it for me any more, nothing I treasured, nothing I believed in. Nothing I could hope for. I withdrew into leaden thoughts like these for the last part of the meal, which made the meal a real low point in our experience together.

Then, as we started breaking up, I turned to Doc and said I had something I needed to talk with him about. In the next instant I heard myself blurting out that I wanted to join the Catholic Church. There were instant exclamations from dear friends around the table but Doc didn't show much reaction. I think he must have smiled a little but he seemed more taken by surprise than anything. When I went further and said I wanted to tell my superior, the pastor of Judson Church, of my decision right away, he counseled that I wait a bit and not rush things. I explained I couldn't wait, that I would not be peaceful until I had made the break complete. Doc said that in that case I should do what I felt was necessary, and the matter was settled. By this time everyone's mood had brightened, not least my own, which by this time was soaring.

I went to see Howard Moody the very first thing next morning and told him of my intention. He, of course, had heard of the special visitor that had been staying with Terry and me. And he knew I had always had a kind of fascination with Catholicism, but he confessed he never took it very seriously; he said he had always thought it more a posture on my part. He was very gracious at the news and at my request I was released from further obligation to the church on the spot. I stepped back into that church only once or twice again, to clean out my desk and to wish Howard a brief and final good-bye. So eager was I to have done with the past.

The day of my conversion is vivid for another reason. It was the day that Hemingway, one of the truly great narcissists of our times, committed suicide. We were walking down Eighth Street right after leaving Howard Johnson's when the news of this came out, spreading like wildfire throughout the Village. I was stunned, for I had admired Hemingway's skills as a writer. I remember Doc looking at me sympathetically, and recall his observing that the way Hemingway chose to end his life was a telling judgment on himself—we heard that he discharged a double-barreled shotgun in his mouth.

Doc later would explain that Judgment Day would be a time of self-judgment. God won't judge us, he said, we will judge ourselves, and our judgments will be true because God will just clap his hands and in that moment we will see ourselves exactly for what we are and what we want. We, not God, would decide our eternal destinies, based on inexorable logic of what it was we spent our life pursuing. The man who has chased false gods all his life will himself judge that he has no place with the true God. God is just, Doc used to say, He gives us what we want. One great and consequential writer had decided what it was he wanted (may God have mercy on him). And, by the grace of God, on that same day so had one small, inconsequential writer, one who prays he will never cease to hope in the Father's Mercy, both for himself and for the likes of him.

> *"For he who finds me finds life,*
> *and wins favor from the Lord;*
> *But he who misses me harms himself;*
> *all who hate me love death."*

The euphoria that came into our lives following the decision to enter the Church is beyond ordinary powers of description. In the Village, our sudden and unexpected decision to enter the Catholic Church created a small sensation, and the peace and joy Terry and I exuded seemed to provoke a reaction almost of envy among many of our friends and acquaintances. I remember telling everyone who cared to listen of my overwhelming sense of no longer feeling lonely. And it was true. I was now an integral part of a family of souls that had been in existence for two thousand years and would continue to exist until the end of time, carrying me along with it. All these souls now were my sisters and brothers.

My conversion produced some minor reverberations outside the Village as well. A cardinal in Philadelphia wanted to meet me, and everywhere I went I seemed to meet priests who had heard of this Protestant minister who converted. Even *Time* magazine sent a photographer down. They had been taking an interest in some of my activities, including an essay I had written for *Exodus* entitled "Postscript for Protestants," and upon learning of my conversion planned to do a story about me. Of course this excited the egoist in me no end. Providentially (for the sake of my humility in those days), someone connected to Judson Church got wind of it and managed to have the story killed.

Meanwhile Doc returned to Mexico and Terry and I took up new quarters in a sixth floor walk-up on the lower East Side. I took an editorial job with Columbia University Press and my little family and I began to fashion what we thought would be a new life for ourselves. But then something happened. We got a call from Doc that he was coming back to New York, on his way to Rome. And he wanted to stay with us. He was being sent to Rome by the Archbishop of Mexico City, to be made a priest. The news stunned us and raised all sorts of new and interesting possibilities. And when he arrived from Mexico, he shared some of them with us, exciting ideas he had for the future of us all. When he returned from Rome as a priest, we would all go to Mexico to form a "house," a community of like-minded where we would learn how to love back the God who loved us so.

Suddenly, there was never any doubt in his mind or in our own that we belonged together for good.

Chapter Three

A New Man

My dear friends,
  if God loved us so
  we must have the same love
  for one another.
No one has ever seen God,
  but as long as we love one another
  God remains in us
  and his love comes to its perfection in us....
Love comes to its perfection in us
  when we can face
  the Day of Judgment fearlessly
Because even in this world
  we have become as he is.
                —I John, 4:11-12, 17

Acquire a fresh, spiritual way of thinking.
You must put on that new man
  created in God's image,
  whose justice and holiness
  are born of truth.
                —Ephesians 4:23f

An organism can only sustain so much change at any given time without it perishing.

ONE AUTUMN SOME YEARS AGO NOW, I bought a twelve-year old Japanese bonsai tree and, following directions, pruned and watered it every day, imagining that by such diligent care this miniature tree over the years would grow in beauty and value and in delight to its new owner. Then winter came and one evening, while fussing with it, I noticed an instruction which said that bonsai trees need a period of dormancy and are best left outdoors during the winter months. So notwithstanding the fact that it was a bitterly cold night, I placed this manicured little treasure outside on the window sill, intending it to stay there until the spring. As you might expect, by next morning the tiny tree was dead.

After all that had happened to us in connection with our conversion, my little family and I must have needed a period of dormancy too. So much in our life had changed: beliefs, feelings, relationships, work, even where we lived (we moved four times in the year Doc was in Rome). These changes actually were all still fairly superficial and easy-to-take compared to what was coming, but God knows how much the soul can handle, even of happiness. For sure He would not put his fledgling plants outside on a wintry night to die. That privilege God reserves for hardwood he intends to season for some special purpose. Doc was hardwood and what God wanted for him now was not unlike a windowsill in winter. It was he, not I, who had now to undergo a time of bitter change. And the man who would emerge from this long night of the soul would not be the same as the person who entered it. That person, by God's design, would die.

1

I DO NOT KNOW WHERE THE IDEA ORIGINATED that Doc should become a priest at this point in his life. Certainly a dream of the priesthood must have lain in him for years, but it was an unrealistic dream, given his age, his marriage, his lack of seminary preparation. As a convert and a Jew not afraid to speak his mind, Doc had always been kept more or less at arms length by the largely Irish U.S. hierarchy, and it was unlikely he could elicit from any of them the backing he would need to promote such a cause in Rome. Then suddenly he found that backing in the person of the archbishop of Mexico City. This prelate had seen something special in the peripatetic Jew who showed up on his doorstep one day, just as we had. We reasoned that if the archbishop could see a priest in Doc, how much more would the very bosom of the Church, Rome, be disposed to recognize and welcome this one-of-a-kind, modern-day apostle. The Pope himself would ordain him virtually on the spot, the moment he realized the truth about him. Of this we had no doubt. Nor, it seems, did Doc.

For us, his spiritual children, Doc's forthcoming ordination was but another step in the unfolding of a divine plan that seemed to be sweeping all of us up with it. After the momentous changes that had taken place so suddenly in our own lives, nothing seemed impossible. We did not know where it was leading us, but as far as we were concerned, this swirl of events was from God and it made us dizzy with excitement and anticipation. God was up to something, Doc was his instrument, and, miracle of miracles, we were chosen to be part of it. We were a motley crew, Doc's Greenwich Village spiritual kids, full of zany ideas, but we loved God as thoroughly as we knew how, loved his magnanimity and believed with all our hearts that perhaps even astonishing things were about to happen, all involving our spiritual father.

The Man I Called Father

For all of us, this virtual summons to Rome was the signal of its triumphant beginning.

We were ten seeing Doc off at Idlewild (now Kennedy Airport) that July evening in 1960. Among the party were several of my Village friends who had lately become attached to Doc—Herbie D., a brilliant young Jewish intellectual connected with NYU who was absolutely fascinated with Doc's mind and for whom Doc had a special fondness; and Gretel C., a used and somewhat weary woman of the Village world who would mysteriously rejuvenate whenever she was with Doc. Present also were the W's, a couple who would later figure very much in our lives, plus of course the usual gang. Doc's mother, Eva, was there too. It was a happy farewell, except perhaps for Eva who never could relate to her son's ways as a Catholic. What was this genius son of hers doing going to Rome, of all things to become a priest? Doc was particularly solicitous for her that night at the airport, I recall, and she seemed graciously resigned to it all, if nothing else. I saw him light a cigarette for her and take one himself, a gesture that must have evoked some ritual from their past together. It was the only cigarette I ever saw him smoke.

Soon as Doc arrived in Rome he began to write letters. I reproduce below the ones that have survived, to my wife, my daughter and myself. As you can see, no one expected his stay in Rome would last more than a few weeks. But already there is a hint that Doc was experiencing a different Rome, one more like the Castle in Kafka's novel of that name, a place of labyrinthine mystery and frustration.

A New Man

Rome, August 9th, 1960
Dear Paul:

Your letter of August 7 gave me great joy. It is so wonderful to see the working of God's grace in your dear soul – and it cheers me so much to know that my children are always closer to Jesus.

I feel you are always close to me too, and I to you – and that we have great things to do together for Him, to bring Him many souls.

I miss you all so much too – but I have felt more and more that this sensible separation is meant to bring us that much closer in the Heart of Jesus.

Kiss Sarah for me, and try to get little things about St. Therese for her. I am sure there's a special connection there, and that the Little Flower's behind her in a most special way.

My plans are still rather indefinite, so I am gong to stay on here for a while, at least another week or so. Sometimes I feel I should get back to Mexico, but then I feel that perhaps I should stay here until I get ordained, maybe get in contact with the Dominicans. I've met the Master General who seems to have taken to me and is helping me a lot. I have a feeling that Jesus would want me to live a kind of monastic life in preparation for my priesthood, maybe with the Trappists, or with the Dominicans.

Paul, He'll show His hand when the time comes. So we'll wait. I'm getting all kinds of graces in the meantime. That's all for now. Please give my love to everyone, to Terry and Sarah, to Howdy and Cindy, Gretel, and especially to Herbie (I loved what you told me about him!)

Devotedly in the Heart of Jesus. Doc

P.S. Any news about Sylvia? I am concerned about her, but I know we'll get her in the end.

Newborn babies must be affected right from birth by the sheer size of their parents, by the way their presence looms over them. The mother's presence of course quickly condenses to intimacy and tenderness. With a father it must be different. From time to time he enters into that intimacy between mother and child but the real world of the father, the child soon realizes, is off somewhere in the primal loom. "Just wait 'til your father gets home" can be the most unsettling words of childhood, not because the father is cruel but because the child glimpses through them that that other world of the father is the one that matters, the one the child must finally come to terms with. It may sound odd nowadays to speak of fathers this way but fathers certainly existed like these at one time in a not too distant world, when families were more intact, when a father was the acknowledged head of his household, when fathers were fathers in the classic sense of chief provider, guarantor of order, and the family's primary link to the world at large.

Doc would return from Rome as such a father (transmuted into spiritual terms) but even from the outset, as you by now know, he loomed large and awesome in the minds of his spiritual offspring. Even if his manner did not yet fully manifest it, he possessed in superabundance the charism of the spiritual fathers of monastic tradition, spiritual masters who exercised authority over their charges as if it came from God, or if you will, just because it came from God. As with any small child in the classic family, such a father indeed represented God to those in his care. It was certainly in Doc's nature to assume authority to such a degree, and indeed, ultimately, he exercised all the authority of an abbot in our lives. But at this stage we were too tiny and Doc must have known that he himself was not ready. Perhaps out of a kind of supernatural deference, while he was in Rome he'd send us letters that instead had all the tenderness of a mother. You can see for yourself how tiny and unimposing he tried to appear to the little family that depended on him and waited in suspended animation for his return. It is as if he knew he too had to become a child, not only for our sake but for his own good as well. These are letters of love and reassurance from a father who was himself a supplicant, and who would shortly experience his own need of consolation. Those of my readers who knew him in later years will perhaps marvel at the picture to be formed of this man here.

Nor could we have realized, at the time, just how deeply we were loved by this man, how gratuitously that love was given and yet how hungry for love in return. We were tiny children, spiritually speaking, partying and enjoying ourselves in endless celebrations of our newfound happiness, terribly proud of the recognition we believed Rome was according our spiritual father, serenely unaware of the trials he instead would have to undergo in the coming year. And in the midst of those very trials, how greatly this man loved the ragged little family he believed God had given him. Even today I still can barely fathom it or account for it. I ask you to ponder it, as you peruse these letters from Rome. Such expressions of love and tenderness, and above all of mutual self-giving, are virtually unthinkable in mature adults who only months before were strangers, unthinkable apart from divine mystery and that vast storehouse of love which, as it overflows, makes trusting, loving children of all who are willing to suffer its force.

2

In the letters that follow, Doc refers to Padre Pio and to the Didos. Let me speak about the Didos first for it was this couple who gained Doc an introduction of sorts to the famous Capuchin monk and stigmatist he had long admired and now hoped to meet. How Doc got to know this couple is unknown to me. They were New Yorkers (the husband was blind) but had the most unusual connections with certain inner circles in Italy. Doc went to see them several times while he was staying with us just prior to his departure for Rome. On one such visit he came back with a carbon copy of a manuscript written by an unnamed nun in Rome who appears to have been a mystic. He placed it in our care, along with some other things from the Didos, and suggested we look at it. It was a most unusual document—recordings of locutions Jesus made to this nun regarding his intention to form a religious community of lay people, a "house" where people from all walks of life, "even sinners," would come to be spiritually formed. They would live together, study the lives of the saints, learn holiness, and then go back out into the world. There was no indication of where this "house" was to be located or when it was to occur. Doc never commented on the manuscript except to agree with us that it was "very interesting." But the document made a forceful impression on me for good reason: since our conversion, Doc had spoken frequently about the "house" that he would form (in Mexico) once he became a priest, and how we would be part of it. This manuscript seemed to be making prophecies about our own future, and perhaps it was, for there are striking parallels between that prophecy and what in fact would happen.

At the time Doc wrote the letter below, Terry and I were taking religious instruction preparatory to our baptism and entrance into the Church, which Doc alludes to and which was not too far off. Our daughter, Sarah, was only five and did not require instruction.

Rome, August 9th, 1960
Dearest little Terry:
I was so happy to hear from you! I love you all in Jesus and Mary, and I will love you forever and ever. I feel that now you are a tiny little baby who cannot do very much except to be loved and taken care of and then you will do whatever Jesus wants you to do because you know you are loved. He knows that you want to give Him everything, but now you are so very very weak, so you mustn't try to do what you can't do, only what He wants you to do, which you will know by keeping close to Him, in Mary, all the time.

And I think too – I learned this from Padre Pio – that He wants you to depend on me, because little babies cannot understand things they don't see and touch. It's as though Jesus and Mary and God the Father are all in me for you now, because I am your father and your mother, just like the mother is to her newborn baby.

So I am sure that Jesus wants you to come to me as soon as you feel disturbed, like a baby crying when it needs its mother. Only you must do it by sending your guardian angel to me, to tell mine that you need help. And all the time, because I am your father and your mother and 'grown-up', in a little way, I am with Jesus, loving Him for you because you are too little to love Him by yourself, and then you know you are being taken care of and loved by Him because He is loving you in me, and me in you.

So! that is your assignment, like a little baby, not to be sad and distressed by yourself, all alone, but to come to me right away, and then you'll be happy because you are being loved and taken care of.

O Terry, if you knew how very, very much you were loved, and how all the defects which disturb you so much are just like a thimbleful of garbage in the ocean, and even that comparison falls short, because enough thimblefuls could make an ocean, but no number of created evils could begin to equal God's Goodness.

Yes, please take good care of that box of Didos' things. Carmella Dido was very worried about it. That's why I wrote.

And about being your Godfather! am I not already that, short of the sacrament. So of course I'll be, to bring my dearest little child, in Jesus, to her Father in heaven, and then we'll be together loving one another as God has already taught us to do, and with Schubert too!

God love you and keep you always. Pray for me, and write soon. I'll be at the above address until further notice.

Devotedly in Jesus and Mary. Doc
P.S. I haven't looked up your friends yet, and I don't think I am supposed to. I need time by myself now, I think.

Rome, August 9th, 1960
Dearest little Sarah:
I was so glad to get your letter, with all the pictures too. And I was so happy because Mommy and Daddy told me how you know all about Jesus, and how much you love Him.

Do you want me to be your Godfather when you get baptized? Because I'd love to, and besides we're twins, and Jesus is going to love us together, and we are going to love each other forever and ever!

So say a prayer to Jesus and Mary for me, and to the Little Flower. I pray for you all the time.

Your Godfather twin, Doc

A New Man

* * *

When Doc came up from Mexico on his way to Rome, he carried with him a little suitcase containing a statue of The Holy Infant of Good Health. This statue looked very much like the Holy Infant of Prague that can be seen encased in glass in many churches, with its white dress, gold crown and scepter, but otherwise there was no direct connection. The statue had been created as a result of Jesus' appearances to a Mexican Indian by the name of Lupita, a disarmingly simple and seemingly very ordinary peasant woman from Morelia. Doc got to know Lupita, and they became friends. Lupita used to tell Doc things that Jesus said about him, some of which were quite extraordinary. Devotion to this Infant spread in the area around Morelia, eventuating in the construction of a large basilica dedicated to The Holy Infant of Good Health. What Doc carried with him was a faithful copy of the original figure housed in the basilica, made, I believe, by the same nuns who fashioned the original. It was Doc's intention to bring this statue to Padre Pio.

Doc had just written us that he was going to see Padre Pio shortly and give him the statue of the Infant. (That earlier letter did not survive.) The letter that follows describes his eventual encounter with Padre Pio.

Rome, Feast of the Transfiguration
Dear Paul:
Your letter was a great comfort to me, and particularly what you said re Padre Pio. Your statement, "I feel that I'll be meeting Padre Pio through you and I'm frankly a little excited, though I don't know why," was amazing. In fact it's far truer than you would ever think. It's all tied up with my experience

with Padre Pio. I hardly know where to start, but I'm sure it's important, very important, so I'll do my best.

Maybe I ought to begin by telling you a little of my experience first, then you'll be able to see what your feeling about Padre means.

Well, it was all arranged for me to have my conference with Padre Pio. The Didos had seen a Commandante Batisti who, I think, is director of Padre Pio's hospital "Casa Sollevis della Soffferenza," a person very close to Padre Pio, the Didos told me. So I arrived in Foggia, the railroad station (about six hours from Rome) Friday nite, July 29th, took the bus to San Giovanni Rotondo, Padre Pio's place, got my room at the hotel. The next morning, as per my instructions, I got up at 4 A.M., went to Padre Pio's Mass, which begins at 5, but you have to be early if you want to be close enough to be able to follow what happens.

The Mass, which lasts about an hour and a quarter, was something of an experience. The chief thing I noticed was that things were happening inside to me, as though an angel were telling me about myself. I wasn't close enough to the altar to follow Padre Pio there. He drops off into profound meditation at certain points, or maybe it's a kind of ecstasy. I'm sure in one way or another he's carried out of himself, whatever it is.

Well, I didn't think too much of what had happened to me. Probably it was, I thought, some light I got in myself thanks to Padre's holiness, or something of the kind. Then I was told to look up a Signorina Lucibelli who would be my interpreter and take me to Signor Batisti, who would arrange the appointment with Padre Pio, at which time I would give Padre the statue of the Niño.

When we entered his office, a huge one on the main floor, Signor Batisti, without ever looking up from his desk, said he was too busy to see me, to see his secretary next door.

The secretary was presumably the devil's advocate who began to ask me all sorts of questions about myself, how old I was, what I wanted to do, whether I wanted to be in an order, *etc. etc. Then he began to say how hard it was to get to see Padre Pio. At this point I suggested that I came because the appointment, I was told, had been arranged but that I could go right back to Rome if it couldn't be. The Signorina Lucibelli was getting more empathetic with me each moment, in fact we have become great friends since. But the upshot of that weird interview was that I was to come back at 11:30 that morning and I would be taken, with the statue, by a certain gentleman, half British and half Italian, who would be my interpreter. So I came back to the office at 11:30 A.M. and met Signor Trevener. Then together we took the Niño, now out of his case, in His royal dress, through the street to the Capuchin Monastery. Then we ascended stairs to a choir where Signor Trevener informed me Padre Pio had received the stigmata some forty years ago, only there was a whole crowd of men who had come to the same place with the same intention, to see Padre Pio.*

And so I realized that this was not going to be a private interview. Only at 12 noon Padre Pio would emerge from the new choir and come to where we were, the old choir, and lead the Angelus. Then, Signor Trevener told me, we would have the chance to speak to Padre Pio and present him with the statue. At that point, I frankly didn't care if I ever saw Padre Pio or anyone connected with him. In fact I was secretly hoping I could have the Niño for myself, but there I was and there was no gracious way of getting away from there. The way persons pursued the poor saint, hounding him at every step, grabbing his poor pierced hands, begging his blessing, trying to kiss his hand, giving him objects to bless, etc. was revolting to me, and I suspect to Padre Pio too. He said once "They'd walk on my head if I let them." And here I was, now, part of this throng.

Well, Padre finally came at 12, said the Angelus, and then tried to get away from everyone, even me!, as fast as he could, which is just what I felt like doing. But then the Signor Trevener couldn't have it that way. So he pursued Padre Pio with the others while I kept lurking farther and farther back, with the Niño, hoping Padre Pio would get away before we met. I just couldn't drag myself after the poor man for one thing, and then I half hoped if this fell though they would be forced to arrange a real appointment. But there was this undaunted Signor Trevener who wouldn't have it that way, and who kept beckoning over the heads of the surrounding people (Signor Trevener is about six and a half feet tall) to follow him. So I did so with much reluctance.

And so we finally caught up with Padre Pio, who by this time wanted only to be rid of everyone. Then Signor Trevener told him about the statue. Padre Pio took a furtive look at me, grunted, allowed me to kiss his hand, told Signor Trevener to put the statue in his (Signor Trevener's house) until further notice, and then he fled to the refectory.

For that I had come some 6000 miles! I thought – but my thoughts, which could quite possibly have become morbid at that sad point, were fortunately interrupted by Signor Trevener who informed me in terms of anxious solicitude and with a thick British accent, "Of course, you know, we've only done half the job!" My interior, but unexpressed reaction to that was, "then Lord deliver me from the other half." But something of what I felt must have got through, because he kept repeating every few minutes or so, "Of course, we've only done half the job, you know! We've only done half the job!"

So we walked towards my hotel, Signor Trevener doing his best to be gracious. Now he was carrying the Niño to his home, while I was trying to see what this was all about. And then, as we parted, Signor Trevener said something like, "You have to be patient you know, have to be patient!" And I muttered, in return, "One can be too patient at times!" and thanked him as I walked to my hotel. (This is getting to be quite a saga. I'll continue with Part II after my siesta)

(Now I not only have had my siesta, but I went to St. John's of the Lateran Gate. It's just a five-minute ride from where I live. I just know I was never made to be a tourist. I'm always glad to get back to my room. After a while you just stop registering, rather I stop. But there is a kind of compulsion you *feel in Rome—so many wonderful things to see, so you feel there's something wrong with you if you're not consumed with a passion to see things. I'm sure that, and so many other things, are wrong with me, but it's just too hot to be very concerned about it.)*

To get on with the story of Padre Pio. I began to reflect when I was alone: Yes, this is the way everything happens to me. It always begins with frustrations, like it did in Rome, and then terrific things begin to happen, when I stopped caring whether they did or not. So, I thought, that's probably what will happen here, and so I almost expected I'd be called at any moment to see Padre Pio. And all the while I was getting more and more convinced that I <u>was</u> communicating with him, without seeing him. It was a strange feeling, as I had said, I think, but you know communication is going on, yet you couldn't say how. It was a little like what happens usually when I write. It feels for all the world that you are just thinking and having ideas, yet you know they are not just your ideas, even though they seem to rise naturally within you.

It was as though my whole life was being laid out in front of me, all the fake, all the corruption, the duplicity, and everything was connected, like having your conscience examined by someone else, and with it there was a great joy, the joy of truth. You realized that the lies were just keeping you from getting the love of Jesus that you wanted. There is something, among many things I wrote while I was there. I think it will give you some idea of what went on:

> *"When you love God, and everything else in God, you are one with the Spirit of Truth. In our hypocrisy we seek the consolation of God's tenderness and love in our lies. But love is strong as death, and the very effect of God's love is to move us to die to ourselves, to ourselves outside of Him, to our lies."*

And again,

"For God to know is to will, to do, and to do is to know. But you, since you are not God, are able to know a truth yet act contrary to it, as Paul says, "The good that I would, I do not." And the danger is that you are inclined, therefore, to take your complacency not in Me, by conforming yourself to Me in action, but to seek your complacency in your understanding of general, abstract truths, which thus become a kind of idol, keeping you separated from Me, and like all idols, justifying sin."

But I couldn't possibly give you an idea of what was happening to me. I was mystified because I have never experienced anything like it, yet I was sure it was happening.

Then Signorina Lucibelli suggested that I go see a Miss Mary Pyle, an American who settled in San Gionvanni some thirty years ago, and who is very holy and very close to Padre Pio. I liked her right away and said something about what I was experiencing with Padre Pio. And then it was like a deluge. She just poured forth all kinds of confirmation of my experience. And then I began to find it in books everywhere, and it all ties up with your guardian angel, and how we communicate with the other, and how God uses our angels in this way to give us grace, and the tremendous power they have, and how we should trust them as we fight against our own evil tendencies.

But what it all comes down to so far is that Padre Pio is my father. I knew he was, but I wrote him a note just to have his sensible confirmation, which he gave me. And that was all I wanted. And now I know he is always watching out for me, and that our guardian angels are always communicating with one another. And the effect of it all is to make me feel very very little, because it is the first time in my life that I feel I have a father. I guess I know what it was to be without one. That was why I tried to be a father to my children, and now it is as if Jesus said, "Look, do you know? You're a child too, and you need a human father, just like your children do." And then what a father He gave me!

And so now you can see why your remark, quoted above, struck me the way it did. Because you know I love you all, and therefore everything I have is yours, including my new father! So he is yours too. And so, whenever you feel distressed by the truth about yourself, as Jesus shows it to you, send your guardian angel to Padre Pio to tell him about it, and you'll see how quickly he takes care of you.

I'm too tired to write more, but I love you all, all, and Terry and Sarah. I'll write to them soon, maybe tomorrow. Pray for me.
Love, Doc

Not long after his encounter with Padre Pio, Doc also got to see the Holy Father, Pope John XXIII. He sent me a picture postcard showing the Holy Father at his desk, poring over what looked like a medieval manuscript. Doc knew a Dominican brother who was part of the Pope's household and so was enabled to roam fairly freely within the Vatican palace. He often spent time in the Pope's private chapel and was sometimes virtually alone with the Holy Father during the Pope's thanksgiving prayers after Mass. I believe the interview with the Pope had been arranged by the archbishop of Mexico City. His commentary on the interview reveals the wry sense of humor he had, basically about himself. The picture alluded to depicts the pope at his deck, reading a manuscript.

Rome, August 18th, 1960
Dear Paul:
Here is a picture of the Holy Father trying to use the time he had to wait for me, to bone up on his theology. You know he'd heard about me! He came out very well in our interview.
Love, Doc

For all the access Doc had to the corridors of the Vatican palace, he seemed not to have any reach into those inner offices where decisions about cases like his were made. He had been in Rome now for over a month with still no tangible progress to report.

Roma, August 21, 1960
Dear Paul:
Your letter of August 11th brought me much joy. I am so happy that you understood what I had written about Padre Pio because now we are that much closer through him. I also appreciate the way you understood, so easily, the meaning of all the delays and apparent frustrations re my vocation. Not that I am preoccupied with any "great" things – but it always works out so that good is brought to myself and very often others through what at first appears to be failure and frustration.

The news about Herbie [D.] is wonderful, although in a way, as you know, it isn't news and it's not strange that a child follows his father – and Herbie is really a child now, and you and Terry and Sarah are children, as I (I hope) am a child – all "twins," all little peas in one pod, and the pod is our Blessed Mother, and Jesus is in her too! with us.

I think that this is about all I have to say now, Paul – except that I love you all and that I think of you and Terry and Sarah very very often. We are really together always. Also, I wanted to tell you that I have a letter from Sylvia, for which I was very thankful. I want so much to help her to see how much she is loved, poor little darling, and I'm sure that is what Jesus wants. It might help if you could, delicately, mention that I had said how much I like her.

Good-bye for now, Paul. Write soon, and keep sending your guardian angel to our father when you need help. Kiss Terry and Sarah for me, and ask them to kiss you for me. I do truly love you, not with my own poor little heart, but with the Heart of Jesus, in Mary.
Devotedly, Doc

P. S. Just got back from another visit with Padre Pio. Things are still going on. I'm sure we've just seen the beginning, and I'll let you know as they unfold. Pray very much for Padre Pio. It's strange how people think he doesn't need prayers, but you have no idea what he goes through.

P.P.S. Terry is most specially in my heart, as she must know. Paul, be most sure of my prayers for her, and assure her. I do love her so very, very much. It's just as if Jesus had brought her to me in His own arms and said, "Take care of my beloved Terry. She is very, very precious to me, and I have great things that I want to do with her." That's really how I feel about her, Paul, and I'm sure she must know it. When I play the piano for her, it is as though we were both two angels in heaven loving one another in Jesus with an eternal love, and praising God for all eternity. She really needs to be loved so very, very much and that is why Jesus gave her to you. So please be filled with confidence. I hope I'll be getting back to you all soon, but I have to wait here to see certain people, and to get definite information about myself re the ordination.

I don't remember if I sent you these pictures of Padre Pio. I love it because I can understand Jesus weeping for us when I look at him. It is probably at the offertory of the Mass where he begs Jesus to receive his offering, sinful as he is, for himself and for the sinners throughout the world.
Love, Doc
P. S. The pictures were blessed by Padre Pio.

From other letters we begin to sense that Doc has entered a time of travail. We see an emerging preoccupation with truth, and we understand that the Spirit of Truth is not an easy master, no more than Doc himself was to be later on. We catch sight of a man beginning to die to himself, spiritually speaking. It is only a glimpse and soon the curtain falls entirely and we are no longer privy to the events of this dark night. Whatever it was that happened, it had to do with Truth, and that experience changed the man who went to Rome and brought back to us a different person.

The Spirit of Truth is also the Spirit of Love. These letters reveal how deeply Doc understood the connection between them, as if to say that there can be no truth for any of us apart from love, for without love the stark truth about ourselves is impossible to bear. As the night darkened for him, we see him reaching out to love, for love, and with love, as if his very survival depended upon it, as we all would come to do, when our turn came.

> *September 13th, 1960*
> *Dearest little Terry,*
>
> *Just to tell you how much Jesus loves you (that includes me!) and to give you another little kiss from Him. (Here follow nine bars of music of a song that Doc composed.)*
>
> *Do you see how He is always telling us to rejoice as little children in His Heart? Dearest Terry, pray very much for your little father — so that he can give Jesus everything — in the Spirit of Truth — like the translucent truth of this picture, when a body is glorified it is all truth. Pray that I may become all truth. Do you know? The secret is for us to love one another, ALL in Jesus, because when you love in Him you become Him, each in the other. How good He was to give me you and Paul and Sarah. Kiss them for me and sing them this little song for me.*
>
> *In the Immaculate Heart of Mary, Father*

* * *

Terry, Sarah, and I were baptized on September 17th, 1961 by Fr. Basil on a Saturday afternoon at the baptismal font in the rear of Our Lady of Guadalupe. Sarah was too little to bend over the font so we held her up and she seemed to want to dive into the basin as Father scooped up the holy water and poured it over her dear little head. Her antics made us laugh. We were all baptized "conditionally" since there was no reason to doubt our Lutheran baptisms had not been valid.

The next day, Sunday, the three of us attended Mass at Our Lady of Guadalupe as Catholics for the first time. By chance we took a pew right behind a contingent of Mexican parishioners who were about to depart on an annual Pilgrimage to the Basilica of our Lady of Guadalupe in Mexico City. I remember the occasion so well because Terry and I received Jesus for the first time! Terry, who was kneeling beside me at the altar rail, told me later that she felt something special had happened during my reception of the Host. I can only speak of the great joy it gave me.

The celebrant, Father Jean Paul, a young Augustinian priest, said a lovely thing during the homily that morning. He asked the pilgrims to pray on their pilgrimage for a "couple that had just been very specially privileged." We felt so blessed at that moment, and indeed in all the days that followed. Terry and I at once became daily communicants, and I remember those next weeks and months as probably the most blissful of my entire life. Many blessings awaited us in the future, but this first season when we were finally able to partake of the mysteries of the Eucharist was like being taken up into heaven.

The "Rosa" mentioned in the letter that follows refers to a woman in Mexico City who had earlier become a devotee of Doc's, and whom we now looked upon and corresponded with as a spiritual sister even though we had not yet met. I call the reader's attention to the words expressed by Rosa's 12 year old daughter, Elisa, which Doc quotes: "Isn't it just great to have a family like ours!" These words should not be taken as the throw-away sentiments of an adolescent. The "family" that she refers to and that was coming into being at this time would have profound reality for its members.

People have criticized Doc for making people dependent on him. This in fact is the classic complaint against him raised by his critics. It is true that his spiritual family became deeply dependent, but not just on him; the fact is we all became dependent on each other. Such was the nature of the spiritual family that Doc envisioned and that actually came to be. Such was the true and authentic nature of the spiritual life as far as he was concerned. Doc said that the saints in the "communion of saints" were like the stones of a Gothic arch, each held in place purely by its union with the stones above and below and without which each would fall. And all the stones were held in place by the keystone which is Jesus Christ. Apart from those relationships, the saint does not exist; saints becomes saints by virtue of communion and never by virtue of what they have in and of themselves. In Doc's mind his critics had simply lost sight of our ordained spiritual destiny. And of course it is true. All one has to do is read Jesus' Last Prayer in the 19th chapter of the Gospel of St. John: ". . . that they may be one as you and I are one, Father, and that they may be one in us." Or to read John's Letters where spirituality and mutual love are virtually one and the same thing. Doc would never agree that this love was merely "intentional," a matter of good will alone. It was meant to be mystical and substantive even to the measure exemplified by Jesus' union with his Father. Doc took Jesus at his word and believed in this special destiny for his spiritual family. It was his stalwart intention then to make of each one of his spiritual children a full-fledged saint, not in the formal canonized sense to be sure, but as full participant in this mystical promise. And that life of union was to begin here and now. "All the way to heaven is heaven," St. Catherine once said. That saying expresses perfectly the agenda of the "house" that Jesus wanted and that Doc built, where I and others lived for twenty years. It was an obscure house but to us who lived there, it was everything.

If the reader wants to understand Doc and the spiritual family that formed around him, read closely the first paragraphs of this letter below. It is the key to everything else that happened. (The 17th was the date of our entry into the Catholic Church.)

Rome, September 28th, 1960
Dearest little Terry:

Thank you for your sweet note of the 21st. As you know I was with you all day on the 17th, and I could never tell you all the joy you and Paul and Sarah brought me that day. How good God is to us, and how much we need to love one another in Him! Yesterday I received the most beautiful letter from Rosa, and I want to tell you something she said because I know it will make you very happy too. Maria Elisa's words [Maria Elisa is her daughter, age 12] 'Isn't it just great to have a family like ours?' have made a very deep impression on me. I think of our little family as a group of children, holding each other's hands in a circle, all pulling up the weak one at the same time, and on and on, until we all together go to heaven. Each one individually has a place that no one else can take, but we are all so very important to the rest and should always be together. This has made me think very much about the Communion of Saints. Every day I turn to the saint of the day for her help on that day. I am so terribly weak that I need the prayers and love of all the saints in heaven and on earth to pull me out, and to receive from them the special graces that they received. I've been thinking that in the godless world this is the time of Communism, and in our Christian world this should be the time of the Communion of Saints. How much, how very much we need each other's love and prayers.

So! my beloved little daughter, do not think that I do not need you, your love and your prayers, just as much as you need mine, maybe a lot more. In fact, it works just that way, because when I realize how much you love me, I find myself loving you that much more. Terry, it is true, we do need one another so much, and I do think that the realization that we are necessary, each to the other, is what dilates our hearts and gives them over to love. Did I ever tell you, or did you read about Mozart, how when all the princesses and royalty were fondling him and making such a fuss about the 'great genius', he turned to one of them and asked "But do you love me: Do you really love me?" That is what Jesus keeps asking at every moment, "Do you really love me?" and that is what each of us is asking, because that is just what each one of us needs, the only thing, to be loved, to be loved, but in Truth, which means to be loved in Jesus, for His Goodness, not for our "own." Yes, because we will never have peace in a love which is based on the illusion of our own worthiness to be loved. Our hearts seek, not only love but love in truth. O, Terry, can you see the wisdom of Jesus' last commandment, why He begged us to love, not Himself, not God, but one another — but "as I have loved you." And that means it has to be all pure, in Him, and yet the love, the very personal love of one another, which lifts us up out of our miserable selves into the very bosom of the Father.

Wasn't it beautiful that you received your first communion together with the pilgrims leaving for Our Lady of Guadalupe? I'm sure it was our Lord's delicate way of thanking His Mother for the gift She had brought Him in you. Yes, She is the new beginning of our life in God, I know, and you, Paul and Sarah are among her first new fruits.

(A long paragraph of personal instruction is omitted here)

Terry, I miss you all as you miss me, so in this too we have to be content with our love of one another in Jesus, in the darkness of this necessary absence. But He is being so good to me here — and everything He gives me is for you and for each one of my children, as you know, and so let us rejoice in the Wisdom and Goodness of our Father.

I don't know whether or not I sent you and Paul a copy of this, together with some other things, but just in case I didn't, I'll copy it again for you here, because I think you will like it. (I think I sent a copy to Howdie, it occurs to me as I write this). Anyway here it is:

> *"O my beloved little child! if only you knew the power of your contentedness, especially when your little heart is breaking with sorrow! If you could see the graces that I pour into your soul then! if you could see the souls you bring to Me then — because you trust in the Love which they have rejected. My beloved little child, give Me at each moment this contentedness of your broken heart in Mine! That is your unceasing act of love. That is the way I want you always, your little heart on My breast."*

Guess that's all for now. Please tell Paul how happy his letter made me and how grateful I am to him for it. I'll answer it very soon. Kiss Paul for me, and Sarah. I loved her music, tell her. It made me think of Ste. Teresa of Avila who was so happy when, after commenting with great facility on the Canticle of Canticles, she came across a line which was all darkness. At first she felt all frustrated — then suddenly she realized that she was cleaving to the darkness of God's word without

any light and how that was more beautiful than all the beautiful thoughts she'd been having.
  All my love in Jesus and Mary, Father

* * *

We would receive few notes from Doc from this point on. There would be no news of progress regarding his ordination. The long night was well advanced and this period becomes a blank as far as we are concerned. I was to learn later that he was sick much of his time in Rome, perhaps from the chronic dysentery he had contracted in Mexico, or possibly from the liver disease that afflicted him in later years and that ultimately caused his death. We know that most of his day was spent in prayer and meditation. He spent hours before St. Cecilia's tomb in the church of her name in Trastevere, the old section of Rome, praying for the gift of purity. Though St. Cecilia is the patroness of music, and despite his own relationship to music, Doc later said he never thought of her in that connection. During the Roman persecutions of the early Church, Cecilia had chosen martyrdom rather than marry an importunate pagan nobleman and thus violate the consecration of her virginity to God. It was for this singular association with purity that Doc remained at her tomb for hours upon hours. I can attest that his relationship to St. Cecilia ran very deep. Twelve years later, in 1972, when with him on a brief visit to Rome, Doc took several of us to St. Cecilia's tomb, down into the excavations deep beneath the church, to the crypt where this saint was buried. Upon kneeling at the railing before her grave, he virtually collapsed with emotion. I recall the moment vividly for I had never seen him affected in such a manner in all my many years with him. I cite this incident because it hints at the sort of experiences Doc must have had during those long months of silence in the winter of 1961-1962. Whatever transpired in those months is hidden away with God, for Doc never spoke of it; but we who lived with him would feel its reverberations in the community that formed around him, for the purpose of being put on the road to sanctity.

> *Rome, December 19th, 1960*
> *Dearest Paul and Terry and Sarah:*
> *This is a time for silence, only to tell you how deep you are buried in my poor little heart with Jesus and Mary, and how grateful I am for all your love, His love in you.*
> *How I wish I could say many things but I guess I can't because little babies can't speak, and this is the time of our Little Baby. But it is true! My love for you is His, all His! That too explains a little, doesn't it, why I can't put it into words. But we are all together in His Heart, in Mary, and that is the way we'll be always, forever and ever.*
> *I am so proud of you! God bless you, and more with each breath and each beat of your dear hearts.*
> *Devotedly in Jesus and Mary, Doc*

Winter would come and go by before we would hear from him again.

> *Rome, April 21, 1961*
> *Dearest little Paul and Terry and Sarah:*
> *Forgive me for not writing. I am sure Jesus doesn't want that now, but you must know how we are always getting closer and closer in His Heart. And you know that everything He gives me is yours as it is mine. I think you will understand, but it is as if anything I write about Jesus now would be a great lie – unless He actually moves me to say something special to a particular person.*

Darlings, I miss you as you miss me. I am alone almost always, but not really. I am always with you in Jesus.

Forgive me for not saying more. You know it is really the Father Who says everything in the Name of Jesus.

Maybe I'll be coming back soon. The archbishop is here in Rome again, and he seems bent on getting things done. He loves me very much, I can tell, and I'm sure he wants me to be his priest. Pray for this, if it is God's will.

Do you know how much I love you. Oh, Paul and Terry, you are my very own, all! I'm sorry I can't say more, but if you could see my poor little heart. We must love one another. That is everything, for ourselves and for the sad, sad world. We must manifest the intimacy, the white intensity, of pure love, His Love, and Mary's, and ours.

Thank you for all your love and devotion. Do you see? I am almost like an idiot. I can hardly say anything. But that is everything.
Devotedly, Doc

Rome, April 29th, 1961 (on the back of a little holy card)
For my darling Paul -
With all the gratitude and love that overflows from my poor little father's heart – for the love and devotion of his son.

The note that Doc refers to in the following letter unfortunately is lost, but the words of this letter manage to sum up in a few sentences the heart of what Doc had learned during his long Roman winter.

Rome, April 29th, 1961
Dearest little Paul, Terry and Sarah:
Please, please meditate very, very much on the enclosed note – and write to me about what happens. I know the Holy Eucharist is the Consummation of everything I have been given to teach – but it is a consummation to be realized by our love of one another in Jesus, in His Sacrament of Love, not by any

words that I might write. The love of our vocation, and especially of our little family, is the Love of God Himself, and therefore it has to be realized in the Word of God. In His Word, in His Word alone, is the Purity of Love for which our hearts so much long. That is how we are, each one, a little host, a little victim of love, dying to ourselves as we give ourselves to Jesus and Mary, and to one another.

O, my darlings! Do you understand? Jesus wants to use us to bring a world dying of diseased love back to the Purity of His Heart, by making us, each of us in his own way, martyrs of the Love of which we die in order to give it to one another. Pray to understand the selflessness of "fair love." "I am the Mother of fair love", because She is the Mother of Jesus, in each one of us, by Whom we love with His Spirit of Love. Devotedly, Doc

The letter below was written on the feast day of St. Athanasius (May 2nd, 1961). It is the last letter from Rome still in my possession.

Dearest Paul and Terry and Sarah:

Excuse the rush, but I wanted to get this to you before going out, and I have to leave in a few minutes.

Chiefly it is to thank you for your dear letter, and for understanding so well what is happening. Yes, it is true, and I think the little note I sent you about the Blessed Sacrament will show you more than anything I could say now about how our love is truly too much for words, because it is the Love of the Word, as the Word is with us in Jesus now, only in His Sacrament of Love. Darlings, we will spend the rest of our lives realizing what that means, and it is such a relief to me to know that all the words I have written have their consummation in the Word. That is the pledge of their faithfulness, and my great consolation, that we are all hopelessly in love with one another, little hosts of Jesus, our family and one host as it is lost in the Great Host. That is our life. Jesus, our Head, is the

Head of an army, an army that defeats its enemies as it dies for them with their Head. But in order to have this generosity and courage we need to be supported always by the <u>human</u>, <u>human</u>, <u>human</u>, sensible love which is a manifestation of the Humanity of Christ, our love for one another which is His Love, His Love in us, yet <u>our</u> love too, in Him.

And so, as I try with each breath to die to Him, all, it is an act of love for you, my beloved little children in Him, and in our Mother. And that, I know, is how you love me. And that is our vocation, to bring back the only pure human love there can be in this mad, confused world, destroying itself with its impurity, because it does not know that the intimacy of human love that it seeks can be found and satisfied only in the Blessed Sacrament. That is everything. Only now I am beginning to see and understand what was behind the terrible revulsion I felt for human words, especially those of "wisdom" and of "love" — now they scream in my ears as unbearable screams of the Anti-Christ.

Thank you so much for the check — it was most welcome — I had actually come to the point of borrowing money for postage!

But, there is one special favor I must ask of you .... [Doc asks us to send his son a birthday present, saying, "It is so important for my children to know that they are loved by me, being so young and my being away, so I know you will understand"]

About my leaving and getting back to the States, right now the Archbishop of Mexico is in Rome and things should come to a head, one way or the other shortly. At times I have the feeling that my enemies may have won the first round, and the answer may be No on the dispensation. But I have been so blessed with graces here in Rome that I am perfectly happy. If fact it might be a sign that God would want me to start some kind of Lay Institute, for which I am quite certain the Archbishop would give her permission, and I hope to take that up with him here in Rome, if the dispensation does not come through. That would mean we would have the chance to get organized and live together in Mexico! But I am certain the dispensation will come along sooner or later. The nature of my vocation is so unusual we must be patient with the authorities who have to follow their own prudence. Sometimes I get scared by the things that are happening. But I know it is right, and it gets confirmed by each one of my spiritual directors who know me inside and out – that is the only way I have of being sure.

So that is all, except please kiss one another for me, and a big hug too, and please do love me – because it is your love that is the Heart that brings the Blood of Jesus to me, and I cannot live without That, really I can't!

Love in Jesus and Mary, Father

None of the letters after this have survived, but they were few in number and very short. He wrote two or three times that he would be coming home in a matter of days but the return kept getting postponed. Gone now was any further mention of ordination now or in the future. I never learned the details of the final outcome, if there ever was one; the impression was that, like the forsaken hero in Kafka's novel, Doc never received an answer one way or the other. It seems they lost his papers, or so it was said. In the end he just abandoned his quest. But another purpose by now had taken its place, for when he returned to us three months later, after a full year in Rome, his manner was that of a man on a mission, acting under orders, a different person altogether from the man who left us twelve months before.

3

It was Monday in early July. The premonition that Doc would return the following Thursday arose in me with such certainty that I called my friends about it. No one had heard from Doc for about ten days, and as there had been several false alarms about his returning, triggered by Doc himself, no one took my prediction very seriously. But by Wednesday, Terry and I received a telegram telling us the flight number and time of Doc's arrival at Idlewild the next day. The moment had finally come! There was no question that Terry and I would be there to meet him, but for various reasons the others could not or would not be present to greet the man we had all said good-bye to exactly one year ago, with what seemed like undying filial devotion.

In those days the International Arrival Building at Idlewild had a glassed-in amphitheater where one could stand and watch the arrivals as they processed through customs down below. Doc's Air Italia flight had just arrived and the three of us, Terry, Sarah, and myself, were there with our noses up against the glass, straining to catch sight of him. We watched as different groups of passengers below straggled out from the bowels of the arrival area. We could see their baggage carts first, then their legs, arms and torsos, pushing their luggage before them, and finally their heads. It seemed to take forever for Doc to thus come into view. Finally there he was, a solitary figure, looking a little more stooped than we remembered. He took a place on one of the baggage inspection lines and then slowly raised his eyes to scan the amphitheater. By this time we were literally jumping up and down, waving our hands. His eyes finally met mine. There was no smile or any gesture of recognition. All I received was a long, probing look that seemed to invade my soul. It changed my mood instantly. My arms fell to my side and all I could do was look back at him and slowly nod my head, as if to answer a question. *Yes, I am for real.*

We made no further eye contact. It must have taken twenty minutes for him to process through the line. Our mood by now had modulated to one of quiet apprehension. As the customs inspector moved to open Doc's bags, we rushed below to be at the door when he came out. We greeted him enthusiastically, as one would expect. His response only confused us. He did not smile. There was no small talk. He barely spoke in fact. We said how glad we were to see him, how glad we were to have him back. We explained how the others of our gang had been unable to come to the airport for one reason or another. His sparse answers to our many questions soon left us with nothing more to say, and we lapsed into discomforting silence. We got into the car and drove back into the city hardly speaking. He asked us if we had eaten and when we said we hadn't, he told me to drive to the lower east side on Delancy Street where we could get something in a Jewish deli. We did all this without really communicating. It was painful and perplexing to say the least. Every so often he would inquire about Howie, or someone else. We tried to act if as nothing had changed, but of course the truth was everything had changed, most of all he himself. Terry and I did not understand what was happening, but those first hours and indeed the next few days were trying. They must have been trying for Doc too, as we re-entered each other's lives, and as he realized the extent of the carnage to his little Greenwich Village family

That first night we went to see Howie Hart. He had done a modern English translation of Paul Claudel's play, *Le Partage de Midi*, (usually translated as "The Break of Noon," though I believe Howie gave it a different title, no longer in my memory) and it was being performed just then in an off-Broadway theater. The play had only recently opened and Howie was at the theater religiously every evening; if we wanted to see him that was where we had to go. We got there early and met Howie outside the lobby. It was an awkward meeting. Doc loved Howie very much, and it was evident that Howie's heart now belonged elsewhere. In the months preceding, during Doc's absence, Howie had been drawn back, little by little, to an old attraction, the lure of "making it" in the world of poetry and theater. The aesthetic life had again become everything to him, an all-absorbing mistress now in the process of swallowing him up; before long we would lose sight of him completely.

Doc and Howie did not speak very much that night. They met once or twice after that also, but it was abundantly clear from that first moment that an unbridgeable chasm had sprung up between this spiritual father and his son. That night in front of the theater I understood that same chasm would now gape between my dear friend Howie and me. Over the next few days this story was repeated with variations of one kind or another with each member of our Greenwich Village gang. Doc had changed, they had changed, and it just wasn't the same any more. The gaiety in Doc was gone, replaced by something deadly serious; and one after another, these friends in Greenwich Village turned away. In each of these bleak encounters, I found myself forced to make a choice of my own as to where I stood. That was the effect this man had on you now: you could no longer opt for both sides of the street.

It was a time of much sadness and soul searching. It was abundantly clear that Doc was a changed man. Gone was the playful humor, the easy tolerance of us and of our weaknesses that he had shown in the past. Gone was the contentment just to be with us, the patience to hear us out and then try to bring us around little by little. We began to realize that Doc was a man gripped by a compelling mission, that he saw everything and everyone in terms of it and that he had time only for those who wanted to join him in it. We did not know what this mission was exactly (except that it had to do with getting close to God), but we understood well enough that this was a time of discernment and decision, that we were all being tested. And in the next weeks, many of those who had once called Doc their spiritual father dropped out of sight. Just as mysteriously, several new faces came into the picture, souls who took their place and who would follow their spiritual father for as long as he lived.

All of this happened out of some inexplicable chemistry between him and the people he dealt with in those first weeks. Doc was not selling anything. He did not explain himself, tell us what his plans were, or try to persuade us of anything. Looking back I would say he was reading souls, trying to discern who was being moved by the Spirit and who was not. Either we belonged with him by virtue of that movement or we did not. But of course it was not that simple, for human choice was a factor too. Each of us understood a choice was being asked of us. There was not much discussion, just a lot of quiet soul searching, each in his or her own way. We had no idea what the future held, what the implications would be of throwing our lot in with this man. I do not think Doc himself knew what the future held in store. But the real issue of course wasn't Doc. The issue came down to our desire for God and whether we would agree to follow his Spirit wherever it chose to lead us. There was no road map, no picture for us to consider in advance. It was as if that Spirit was asking each of us to sign a blank check. It turned out that few were detached enough from their own agendas to risk that much.

4

When Doc returned from Rome, Terry and I were living in a cheap rented apartment on Grand Street on the lower east side, a sixth floor walk-up comprising four small rooms. It had been a hot summer and our apartment unfortunately was right under the roof. An animal of some kind, probably a rat, had recently died beneath the floorboards of our tiny bathroom and for a while the stench in that part of the apartment was virtually unbearable. Happily at night there always seemed to be a breeze – at that height we could open all the windows without fear of mosquitoes and moths. This usually cooled things off and freshened the air. Doc began staying with us and never seemed to notice these problems.

I said earlier that Doc was not selling anything, was not trying to persuade us of anything or get us to do anything. It was hard to figure out what he was up to, and probably he himself did not know. As I said, it seemed to be a time of discernment for all of us, waiting for the Spirit to show its hand. And indeed some very telling things happened in those next few weeks. There was a series of small, very personal episodes that I share with you now, so that you may see how the Spirit was preparing one of the characters in this drama for the future we had in store, an obscure future as far as the world was concerned, but one that would profoundly change the private, spiritual lives of those who were swept up in it.

Doc had been back perhaps about three weeks. On this particular day he was over in a nearby town just outside the city, visiting the W's. Father D., a Dominican priest and disciple of Doc's was also staying with us just then and was with him that night. Terry and I were alone with Sarah in our sixth floor walk-up, not knowing what to do with ourselves. We didn't speak much about our private thoughts, but I recall suddenly saying to Terry that I had come to a momentous conclusion about Doc and that I needed to talk to him. In the next instant I was on the phone to the W's, speaking to Doc. I said words to the effect that I had something very important to tell him when he got home. Later that night, when he and Father D. returned and he was settled by the open window of our small living room, he looked over at me. *You said you had something important to tell me. What's on your mind?* he asked. I leaned forward and said, *I had a great realization today: I realize I need to be under obedience to you.* Doc did not seem impressed. He looked at me for an instant. *All right,* he said finally. *You can go to Father Basil.* I was a little stunned at this. It had seemed like such a momentous step for me, and here he was seemingly turning me down and passing me off to someone else. But then I realized in the next instant that Doc wasn't Father Basil; he was testing my disposition to obey, and I had the grace – the good sense – to give more or less immediate assent to his suggestion as my first act of obedience. The truth is we never spoke of the matter again; but I had declared myself and the message seemed to have registered, both here and in heaven.

Not long thereafter, the Dominican priest, Father Basil, came to visit Doc and the three of us went out for dinner. Doc and Father Basil were very close and had had a long relationship that went back to the days when Doc used to visit the Dominicans priests and seminarians at their House of Study in Washington D.C. Father Basil was Doc's confessor and Doc regarded this priest with special affection and devotion, which Father Basil just as readily returned. Although Doc was his junior, Father Basil deferred to him in virtually everything outside of the confessional. But essentially they were peers: both men were steeped in Thomism and they enjoyed each other's conversation immensely. That evening at the dinner table, as their talk ranged from one topic to another, I recall feeling a little like the odd man out. I could barely follow their conversation at times and I began to wonder what I was doing there. I began to feel rather miserable in fact. Then something very strange happened. It started as a warm, comforting feeling rising up in my heart and gradually becoming a flood tide, and ended with an extraordinary experience of interiorly communing with Doc, as if our two inner selves, our hearts, were coming together to occupy the same physical space. He was still engrossed in conversation with Father when this all began to happen to me, but then suddenly he turned and looked at me and smiled. I cannot even begin to describe what was going on inside of me just then, but what it communicated to my mind was a deep and profound commingling of my spirit with that of my spiritual father. When he turned to look at me it was clear he knew and understood that something was happening between us. The feeling seemed to intensify and Father Basil also became aware that something special was happening. In the next instant we were all sort of smiling and blushing happily. I had never experienced intimacy with another person like that before. It was nothing like the intimacy of marriage. This was spiritual and more completely interior, yet at the same time somehow physical too; at least it had a physical affect. It seemed to wash over the three of us, but it had to do just with Doc and me. After a long moment, the conversation picked up again but now I was part of it, perhaps even the heart of it. Doc said something nice about me, I recall, and Father Basil looked over at me with love in his eyes. The rest of the evening is a blank in my memory: all I know was that I was miserable one moment, and in the next, immensely and unaccountably peaceful and happy.

This was the first time anything even remotely like this ever happened in my life. I would often again have a sense of interior connection with Doc over the next twenty years but only three or four times did I ever again experience anything quite like that first evening. Oddly enough – this circumstance only just now occurred to me – with possibly one exception, what took place subsequently always took place also in the presence of a good and holy priest. I have no idea why a holy priest should have almost always been present during such moments, but perhaps it is God's way of reassuring me when I would sit down and write about this many years after the event, when such phenomena in retrospect might be questioned.

An even stranger thing happened between Doc and me one night during the time he was staying with us upon his return from Rome. Terry and I had gone to bed a bit early and were asleep in our bedroom just off the living room. I had been asleep maybe about an hour or so when I was suddenly startled by a terrifying image of someone I was very close to, someone who meant very much to me. I saw this person in hell. I knew it was hell by the person's eyes. They were singularly large round eyes made of shattered glass, peering out at me in hopelessness and despair. The image of that face was so vivid and real I uttered a long, loud wail. I lay there for a minute or two half-awake by now, stunned by what I had seen. Suddenly Doc appeared in the doorway and whispered my name. *Are you awake, Paul?* he asked. *Come out here for a minute,* he said when I responded. *I want to talk with you.* I got up. I was groggy and still overwhelmed by that hideous dream as I dragged myself into our tiny living room. Doc was sitting by a lamp. I took a seat and we just sat there in silence for a while. I was barely able to focus my mind. And then Doc said simply, *You really are my son, aren't you Paul.* I nodded and merely said, *Yes.* I could hardly keep my eyes open. I think that's all we said. I was dead inside, unable to feel or say anything more. After a long silence in which no one spoke, Doc said gently, *Go back to bed. God bless you, Paul.*

I did not tell Doc of this vision until one evening fifteen years later when we were discussing the person I had seen in my dream that night. As I recall, this individual was in a particularly precarious state at the time of this later conversation. Doc listened carefully to what I had to tell him and, after a pause, said that it sounded right to him. I took his remark to mean that in some way the dream had had a supernatural origin, which I had always felt was the case. We didn't talk about it further and I am not free to tell you anything more about the individual in that vision or dream or whatever it was, except to say that this person today, thirty-five years later, is spiritually alive and well, and if I am any judge, securely in God's hands and well on the way to an eternity with Him. I am as certain of that as any human can ever be of such matters. Of all God's mercies alluded to in this book, nothing moves me to gratitude today nearly as much as the mercy that has since been shown to this particular soul.

5

I was now Doc's spiritual son without equivocation, and very soon (it seemed to me) the mood changed in our little group. Doc began to regain some of his former liveliness, and the sense of our being a little band of Christian souls united for reasons as yet unknown, but truly united, overtook us and we became happy and peaceful again, if not what you would exactly call carefree, as it was in the past. Doc's family now was fewer in number and some of the faces were different, but if anything we were more bound to each other than ever, perhaps in the way soldiers are who have recently survived the fire of battle. Interestingly, Terry, and

Sarah too, did not appear to have any problems with what was happening; it seems they just fell in with everything, as if they had been there all along.

The fact is it was no longer possible to take up with Doc simply by laughing at his jokes and going along with his line of thinking, the way it was before. It would now cost you something to know this man, and anyone naively wishing to do so would soon discover they were getting into considerably more than they bargained for.

Let me tell you of one such instance.

The W.'s came to see Doc at our sixth floor apartment one evening in the company of another Catholic couple, Clifford and Paula C., who had never met Doc before. Both had large families. Tom W. was a military analyst at an important think tank, and his friend, Clifford, was a mathematician. Clifford had said he'd like to meet Doc when Tom spoke of him during lunch one day.

There were eight of us in our cramped living room that night: Doc, Father D., Terry and I, Tom and his wife Jane, Clifford and his wife Paula. After the introductions, I offered Paula a seat (as I recall she looked a little weary). Doc sat down across from her. For some reason, probably because there were not enough seats for everyone, most of us drew back against the walls, leaving Doc and Paula center stage. What transpired next had almost the property of a drama.

Picture the scene if you will. On the one hand we have this unsuspecting housewife who accompanies her husband on a social visit. She is in her mid-to-late thirties, the mother of six children, and apart from looking a little tired that evening, gave every appearance of being a wholesome, quintessential Catholic suburbanite. If you would ask her parish pastor, he would doubtless say of her that this is the stuff parishes are made of. Across from her, for the next two hours, sits this intense individual recently returned from Rome, his eyes never leaving her. There is no small talk. He begins immediately by asking her to tell him about her faith. Her hesitant answers aren't too articulate; like most of us, probably no one had ever questioned her about her faith before. Doc, of course, was gentle with her, but unrelenting at the same time and would not let her off the hook. His questions were never harsh, not in the least. It was clear he was really trying to understand her, what made her tick spiritually, as if he were trying to grasp his own possible role with Catholics like her. But his interest in her, genuine as it was, was clearly making her uncomfortable. The more they spoke, the bigger Paula's eyes became, and the more electric the atmosphere in that room. It was not long before each of us was privately grateful it was someone else undergoing this examination.

Paula C. happened to be Doc's first encounter since returning from Rome with what you might call a prototypical Catholic. The characters in the Village that he had been dealing with up to now were hardly representative of American Catholicism. But now before him sat an ordinary church-goer, if I may say so, the kind of Catholic who in those days filled the middle pews of the Roman Catholic churches in America every Sunday – someone faithful in attending Mass, faithful about going to confession, assiduous in avoiding serious sin, in keeping the fast days, and so on, but not one of whom it could be said was particularly aware of the interior life of faith and of the intimacy with God that such a life entails. In those days, ordinary Catholics generally believed that such intimacy was reserved for clerics and religious, those who were called to go the whole route, spiritually speaking; this was not felt to be the calling of suburban Catholic housewives. But as I have been explaining, Doc didn't share that point of view. And now he had sitting before him a lovely representative of modern American Catholicism, with an opportunity to explore his own vocation with respect to such souls. The opportunity proved irresistible. It was as if an immense backlog of pent-up reflection and feeling about the state of modern everyday Catholicism erupted in an uninterruptible flow of probing questions. Not that Doc harangued her in the least, or preached to her. His method was strictly Socratic, but fairly relentless for all that, plying her with questions that led to other questions that in the end clearly begged their answer and left their victim feeling spiritually unclothed.

I wish I could replay their conversation but my memory draws a blank. It was obvious Doc liked her, and that he respected and thought well of her. But all I recall is the pale look of alarm spreading across Paula's face, and the somewhat sheepish grin on the faces of us men as we hung to the background. Yet the evening ended well, with laughter and abundant good spirits, even if Paula could not quite shake that rather shell-shocked look in her eyes. No matter, a spiritual work was begun that night. Over the next years, the C's would be led into far deeper spirituality, Paula most especially.

At times like this Doc was discovering his own vocation since returning from Rome, to shunt Catholics of all varieties off a broad, meandering roadway onto a straight, narrow path that could one day lead to sanctity; a prospect, it might be said, that was being held out to everyone in that room that night.

6

Doc called me aside one day not long after this and said he had something he wanted to discuss with me. He explained that when he was in Rome his vocation had become clearer to him and that what he felt he was being called to do was to gather together people who wanted, as he put it, "to go the whole way" in the life of faith. He said that this life of faith was consummated by union with others in Jesus. This union, he said, was not just friendship, identity of purpose (intentionality), or anything that superficial, but had to do with the very substance of our being. He said Christians were called to participate in *substantial* union with each other, a union just as real as that which Jesus had with the Father. We were called to be *one*, as Jesus and the Father were one; our union with each other was to be a literal participation in *their* union. Our lives as Christians meant we were no longer a single entity on our own. We did not go to God as soloists, we went in union with others, especially with those who prayed for us and for whom we prayed. But it wasn't just that we related to others, spent time with them, prayed for them, shared their purposes, their interests, their beliefs, and they ours. It was union in its most profound and intimate sense, a union of substances, far more intimate in fact than marital union. He said it entailed a kind of letting go of personal autonomy, an entering upon true dependency on God and on other members of the mystical body, much like the way the stones of a gothic arch depend on each other and would fall without the support they receive from each other and most critically from the keystone at the apogee, which symbolizes Christ. Thus we who make up the Body of Christ are not autonomous albeit cooperating parts, but members in intimate, organic dependency upon our Lord who is our Head and upon each other. Without this union we are isolated and stillborn, spiritually speaking. Without this support from each other, spiritually speaking we collapse.

Doc then asked me what I thought about what he had said. I reflected for a few moments (I realized this was a litmus test and that I might not do well with it), and then I said frankly that this notion of an intimate union of substances made me think of those aberrant religious communities in the Middle Ages that practiced sexual license. I had read about such phenomena in my Protestant seminary studies. l said maybe spiritual intimacy like that could lead to similar sexual disorder. He nodded but happily didn't comment on my misgiving. I quickly added that I also had a real sense of what he was getting at. I told him about my own experience shortly after getting married, about the feeling I had had, that Terry and I had ceased to be separate individuals and that a new reality had overtaken us, of our being a "we," and that this new entity was fundamentally different than that of two single people linked together in some way. I told Doc that in the first few months of our marriage we used to celebrate this "we" like a great spiritual discovery, or at least it was one that I felt. I said I once spoke about it to a good friend of mine, a pastor at a Lutheran church in Brooklyn (who has since become a practicing psychiatrist) and who as far as I could tell was happily married to a very fine, intelligent woman, and how it struck me when he said he couldn't really relate to what I was telling him. I also told Doc that this sense of "we" quickly vanished as difficulties arose in our marriage.

Doc seemed to like what I was telling him, but oddly enough that was the end of it. I never heard him speak of this in such plain terms again. Perhaps he spoke to others privately, as he had to me. But I never heard him say such powerful things again in so many words. Perhaps because they were too easily misinterpreted. Or perhaps because the reality wasn't in the words or the ideas but in the living, and this was what he set out to do. Or perhaps his thinking on this subject underwent change. All I know is that a small community that embodied these ideals, at least to some degree, sprang up around him and lasted over twenty years. And I know enough about classical Christian mysticism to understand that his thinking here, radical as it seemed, was rooted in ancient tradition. Jesus had prayed to his Father for this union among his followers. This prayer of Jesus is echoed throughout the Epistles of St. John, the disciple whom Jesus loved, and who saw an inseparable link between our love of God and our love for each other. John taught that this love was made both possible and imperative for us because it had its origin in the love God revealed to us in his Son. Our union with Jesus, and with each other in Jesus, is the end to which God's love is leading us. Strange how rare it is for anyone nowadays ever to allude to this, to *substantial union* as being the end to which we as Christians are destined. We are all like sleepwalkers in this regard, acting as if Jesus had never prayed that such things might be true of us, his followers. Who nowadays can relate to it?

Doc once said that the great councils of the Church have defined all the important truths of the faith with but one exception. We have the great doctrines of the Trinity, .the Incarnation, the two natures of Christ, the place of Mary as Mother of God, the Immaculate Conception, the Assumption of Mary, and the Infallibility of the Vicar of Christ as head of the Church. The one exception, he said, relates to us baptized believers. There has been no formal pronouncement about us and the mystery of our new life in Christ, what it means to be baptized, to become a follower of Christ and a member of his Mystical Body. I believe St. Augustine wrote somewhere that if we really understood who we are as Christians, we would fall down in adoration at the sight of each other, because in baptism we have received a divine nature.

Perhaps formal pronouncements about us as Christians cannot be made because, as long as we are in this world, nothing can be presumed about our destiny. We are on a spiritual journey, and that journey is precarious at best; what was given in baptism can be lost. We must "fight the good fight," St. Paul said, so as not to lose our privilege. Caution and prudence suggest, then, that we not aim too high or presume too much. Nevertheless there was this man who took Jesus very literally and who aimed high, not only for himself but for those willing to stick it out with him.

7

Doc returned to Mexico City a few weeks later. Before he left, however, we received a visitor from Mexico from a devotee of Doc's by the name of Rosa. She was in her mid thirties, of Spanish lineage, and was very beautiful and very devout. Rosa had gotten to know Doc some years before, soon after he had arrived in Mexico City, and had instantly attached herself to him. She seemed ahead of us, spiritually speaking, and as our community began to take shape, Doc relied on Rosa as a spiritual partner in his work with souls. Rosa and I would grow close later on but in those first days our relationship was somewhat distant, or so it seemed to me; I felt unable to make real contact with her somehow. I found it a little frustrating in fact.

Rosa had hardly been with us a week when, one afternoon, Doc suggested he and I go for a little drive. He asked Rosa to come with us. We got into the little Renault I had at that time and drove around the lower East Side until Doc asked me to pull over somewhere and park. He began very delicately to explain he had something to tell me about myself and that I should say a prayer I would be open to the truth. He then observed that I had a very deep problem in my relationship with my father, that my relationship to him in fact was not a good one. I immediately interrupted him to protest that he must be mistaken: I loved my father and had always had a good relationship with him. Doc tried to continue but I simply could not relate to anything he had to say. He told me to give the truth a chance but all I did was become upset, protesting that what he was saying about me simply wasn't so. I loved my father and respected him immensely. At this point Rosa broke in as if to defend me, but Doc cut her off. I felt that I was being attacked, criticized without justification, that my good nature was being unfairly questioned, and a sudden fear seized me that something about Doc was not right, that he might be unbalanced. The whole episode struck me as crazy, redeemed only by Rosa's wanting to come to my defense. From that moment on I began to feel very differently about her. But as for Doc's talk that afternoon, all it did was unsettle me. Doc didn't pursue it any further. He just said I should think about it, that I would see the truth if I gave it half a chance. I nodded somewhat sullenly that I would try and we drove home in silence, with me having a sour taste in my mouth. Doc seemed immediately to forget about the whole affair, and in a day or two the matter receded from my mind as well. I had not tried to understand the things Doc told me; in the final analysis the episode made no impression on me whatsoever, not at the time at any rate. It would take much deeper surgery before Doc would manage to cut away the fiction of my life, before I could acknowledge negative things about myself, before I could begin to have misgivings about myself instead of him. In the meanwhile, I put such unpleasantness out of mind.

* * *

When Doc (and Rosa) left us to return home to Mexico City, no one had any idea when we would see each other again. I had a job in Manhattan and needed to stay right there to support my family. There was no longer any talk of our coming down to Mexico, of forming a "house" there of some sort, or of his coming back to New York.

We understood we would see each other again but we had not the slightest inkling when or under what circumstances.

My first reaction to all this was to move out of the lower East Side back to Greenwich Village into a nice ground floor apartment with a little backyard patio. We gave up any notion now of journeying to Mexico, and with that realization, our year-long existence as virtual gypsies came to an end. We had lived in four different places while Doc was in Rome, expecting to relocate to Mexico the moment he came back as a priest. Now it looked as though we might as well settle down and get on with our lives.

Settling down and getting on with our lives lasted all of a month before Doc was back with us. It happened this way. My conversion had attracted some small attention among clerical circles in the New York archdiocese, and one day I received a telephone call from a priest who was the Catholic chaplain at the NYU campus in the Village. I had heard of him during my days at the Protestant church and knew him to be friendly and easy-going. He explained over the telephone that he would like to get together and so we arranged to have dinner at an Italian restaurant in the Village. The dinner meeting with this priest was extremely pleasant. The priest – whose name is now lost to me – said he had wanted to get to know me and to discuss the possibility of our doing something together. He explained that the archdiocese had a modest amount of money that he could probably lay his hands on for the kind of things he had in mind. Perhaps we could put out a publication, he speculated, alluding to the sort of things I had done while at Judson Memorial. I saw this as an opportunity to tell him about Doc. He took it all in in what I thought was a very good spirit, and when I finished, he reflected that maybe Doc could also have some part in these activities. We parted on very good terms. He was going to pursue this with the Chancery, and I would write Doc and inform him of our discussion.

Looking back on it now, the evening had not really gone that well. I undoubtedly had taken this priest's notions in a direction he had not foreseen, and though he seemed open to it, his enthusiasm must not have run very deep or been very real. No matter, for it all served a good purpose. I wrote to Doc about the encounter and he wrote back at once saying that it might be a sign, and that he would be coming up shortly to meet this priest, which is exactly what he did.

There were four of us at the restaurant the night of this meeting: this priest, Doc, the Dominican priest Father D. and myself. The evening turned out to be a big nothing, as flat as it could possibly be. Nothing seemed to gel at the personal level, and when I broached the main subject, this priest seemed evasive, mentioning something about not being really sure if that money was available, and so on. It didn't take much for the three of us to realize there was nothing doing here, and the dinner wound up being short and utterly anticlimactic. But as I said, no matter. In encouraging Doc to come up, I had written that he could stay with us indefinitely. So Doc was now in New York with all his belongings, few as they were. If our expectations had gone awry, God surely had his own ideas. And indeed, Doc and I were fated to be together from this point on until the moment of his death nineteen years hence.

It was not human affection that brought us together this way. This was not a case of two people who liked each other so much, who clicked together so well, that the two could not keep themselves apart. That would not characterize our relationship in the least. Nor was it human calculations and dreams of accomplishing some important work together. We never ever talked in such a vein. After Doc moved in with us in our small Village apartment, life went on much as it had before. I went to work every day, Doc spent the day with Terry and Rosa who had by now also joined Doc as our house guest. In the evening we often had visitors, particularly the W's who lived just outside the city. Or we went to visit them. Apart from our simply being together, we had no plans or projects. Doc simply did not see life in terms of enterprises, as a matter of *doing*. When most people meet, they ask, *And what do you do?* as if in knowing how a person spent his day one knew that person. On that basis, Doc and his little family has little to say for themselves. And yet important things were happening all the time in the order of *being*.

You must remember that Doc offered his life as a single-minded instrument of God. He did not come to us as a friend exactly, but rather as an emissary, as an instrument of a divine purpose he himself probably only grasped in barest outline – to bring souls more deeply to God. Wherever he went, whomever he was with, Doc applied his mind and his energies to that single end, and to that end alone, to draw souls into a deeper relationship with God. Except, that is, for some infrequent occasions when it seemed he allowed himself the liberty of just being himself, almost as if without reference to God (i.e. the way most of us are most of the time). As I said, it did not happen often, usually at moments of fun and relaxation, like when he would suggest we play a board game together. Perhaps he turned to such games when he did not know what else to do with us. Anyway, during such times he seemed to became another personality, as if the fact that it was only a game made it permissible for him to let go of God and give his own strong nature free play. This at any rate was how it seemed to me on more than one occasion. It was on just one such an occasion, when Doc was "being himself" that I almost walked away from him, as someone I positively loathed.

It happened this way. We had gone to the W's for the evening. At some point we began to play a game of Monopoly and suddenly I found myself playing against a man who struck me as crude and ruthlessly overbearing, to the point of being boorish. It was not just that he wanted to win, but he used his considerable powers of persuasion and intimidation to gain advantage at every turn. Probably he affected me this way because I wanted to win every bit as much as he and far more than I should have. The others just took the game as great fun and seemed to be enjoying his antics immensely; but as the play progressed it began to turn my stomach. My loathing became so strong that I had to excuse myself from the game. I went to the bathroom and in desperation splashed cold water on my face. I felt such revulsion I didn't see how I could go back to the party, how I could face him feeling as I did. What was happening to me? I sensed I was being tempted but I couldn't tell where objective truth left off and temptation began. I recall slapping my face over and over to free myself from the grip of this loathing. I was terrorized because beneath all this emotional turmoil I sensed some great issue was at stake. I got down on my knees and begged God for grace to not despise Doc, grace to not walk away, grace to get through the evening without incident.

I somehow managed to go back into the game and to survive the rest of that evening without calling attention to myself. But the next morning I was no better. The loathing was still there like a knot in my stomach. Doc and Rosa had gone out early somewhere with Sarah and I remember asking Terry out for a walk. I told her I was thinking seriously of breaking with Doc. I didn't say what was bothering me about him, just that I was having strong second thoughts about everything. I gave her some rambling explanation as to why I thought this was the right course for us, or at least for me. She looked at me without sympathy and I soon realized I had no ally in her.

I next did what I later always came to do when difficulties arose between Doc and me. Soon as he and Rosa returned, I told him about the whole affair, about what transpired the previous evening, down to the detail of repeatedly hitting my face in the bathroom. As I was saying this, he reached out and struck me across the face with considerable force. He didn't say a word, but I held my head in my hands and walked away into the other room. A moment or two later I let out a deep, loud wail – I think some psychiatrists call it a "primal cry" – coming from the sub-sub-basement of my psyche. For a few moments all I could do was sob. I don't know what I was sobbing about. It had nothing to do with physical pain, but the psychic pain was almost unbearable. I think I must have been alone in that room for maybe twenty minutes or so, head in hand, unable to reason or even move. The rest of the house was still as a morgue. Then Rosa came in and sat by me. She didn't say anything at first, just a few words of sympathy and reassurance that everything would work out all right. Then she added that I shouldn't worry, that I would be forgiven. I looked at her in amazement. *Me* be forgiven? What had *I* done wrong? But I looked at her again and saw someone loving me. I glimpsed then, just barely, that it just might be so – *I* was the problem, not Doc. And with that half-glimmer of recognition the conflict in my heart and mind began to lift. My face must have communicated that the crisis was over because Rosa put her hands on mine and told me I should feel myself very lucky. *It usually takes monks and nuns ten years to learn what you learned today,* she said. I didn't really understood what she was talking about. I was just grateful that the knot in my stomach was gone and that no irreparable rupture had occurred between us. It would take me a while before I could see that something really good had happened.

Earlier in the summer Doc had tried to get me to realize I had a problem with my relationship to my natural father. I rejected the suggestion out of hand; I simply couldn't see it. But now it was pushed in my face that I had had a colossal problem with my spiritual father. And that the problem wasn't so much him as it was *me*. Why else had no one but me had such reactions the previous evening? I still had no idea what might be wrong with me, but at least now I began to have some faint misgiving about myself. This was the good that was accomplished: the doubts I had had about Doc I now began in some small measure to have about myself. It was just a beginning, just a little shift, but an important first step in the rehabilitation of a psyche and the freeing of a soul.

I have no idea whether you, the reader, can relate to the foregoing. Perhaps you never have a problem with authority. Perhaps you are not a rebel at heart, or maybe you too have simply never acknowledged it. I was a rebel in spades and I know I still am to a great extent. Except that now I *know* this truth about myself and I also know what to do about it, along with some other things in my character. My reactions that evening had to do with resisting Doc's dominion, symbolically fought out in a silly game of Monopoly. I didn't want this man dominating *me*, no more than I allowed my natural father to hold sway over me. In my father's case he didn't even try, which may be precisely why I come to disregard authority in the first place. But the crucial point here is not rebellion or its causes, but our resistance to truth. We fight against seeing that there is anything wrong with us, and we resist with all our strength any such suggestion from others, as if our peace of mind depended upon it, which of course it usually does. Who among us can take criticism, particularly criticism that gets perilously close to home? Humanly speaking, I suppose the most we can hope for is that we be touchy but truthful.

One of our most predictable reactions to criticism is to suspect that something is not right with the person fingering us. What's *his* problem? Who does s*he* think *she* is? Doc used to say if we want a clue to the personal defects we are hiding from ourselves, just pay attention to the things we are quickest to notice and criticize in others. Chances are these very faults are our own as well, which is why we pick them out so readily in others. We want to think these faults are *theirs*, not *ours*.

* * *

So Doc was finally getting someplace with me, although you'll notice that he spoke hardly a word and that the whole episode was principally God's work: Doc's role was limited to the back of his hand, and a lot of prayer no doubt. In any event, our relationship improved after that, became simpler, more real, more truthful. He told me once I had a spirit of truth and that this was my salvation, and perhaps it is so. There would be many ups and downs and things at times would get worse in my relationship with this man (and with God, I might add) before they really got better. But I can say from hard experience that confession, truthfulness before one's spiritual authority, is *always* at the heart of spiritual healing.

Doc had returned from Rome a new man. And now he set about making new men and women of those who dared to stick it out with him. It would not take place if you didn't want it to happen. If you didn't know in your heart of hearts that you were a failed human being in some deep respect and needed to be remade as a person, if you didn't feel you needed to change and knew there was no way you could do this for yourself, if you didn't believe that all that was happening to you now was coming from God, that Doc was God's big chance for you to be renewed as a person, to become *His* child, one with whom He too could be well pleased.

A New Man

*You must put on that new man
created in God's image,
whose justice and holiness
are born of truth.* (Eph. 4:23-24)
*. . . because even in this world
we are become as he is.* (I John, 4:17)

* * *

IT WOULD TAKE ANOTHER SEVEN YEARS living under the same roof with my spiritual father before it could be said that I became a new man. How this came about is another story, but one not so very different from the one told in these pages, only considerably more intense perhaps. Nor was the way it ended very different from the way it started. To repeat T. S. Eliot's dictum, our end is in our beginning and our beginning is in our end. So what God started way back when, one day, this man we called Doc came into our apartment in Greenwich Village and we exchanged looks for that very first time, would come to an end 20 years later in just that way. The morning that Doc died, I was by his bedside in the hospital. He had lain incommunicado for several days, but then, just at the last moment, he rolled over and faced me and the few others who were there, and with his eyes barely inches from my own, I saw him pass away to the One he had loved and sought to serve with everything he had been given.

Chapter Four

LIBERATION

In 2001, at the Buenos Aires International Book Fair in Argentina, Cardinal Bergoglio (Pope Francis) gave a talk that really hit home with me. Let me quote what he said:[1]

> Everything in our life, today just as in Jesus' time, begins with an encounter. An encounter with this Man, the carpenter of Nazareth, a man like all men and yet different. The first ones, John, Andrew, and Simon, felt themselves to be looked at into their very depths, read in their innermost being, and in them sprang forth a surprise, a wonder that instantly made them feel bound to Him, made them feel different.

You can probably see why this remark struck me. It was my encounter with Doc that eventually brought me to the precious encounter with Christ described so aptly by the Pope. The experience of meeting Doc and knowing he saw me to my depths

---

[1] These quotes are from Moynihan, Robert, *Pray for Me: The Life and Spiritual Vision of Pope Francis*, p. 170f. Image (New York), 2013.

was not unlike what the apostles must have felt on encountering Christ. It was that life-changing. As you know by now, the relationship with my spiritual father lasted twenty years, and over that time Doc got to know me inside and out. He certainly knew the worst about me too, and yet for all that, he never ceased to treat me as a much-loved son. Understandably, there were ups and downs in our relationship, and as a spiritual father he was sometimes tender, sometimes tough. Like any good father, spiritual or otherwise, he wanted my best. But what he wanted most for me was that I be truthful. To him, truthfulness was the *sine qua non* foundation to any spiritual achievement; as far as he was concerned, there was no true spirituality without it. And we were not to be afraid of the truth; the truth is your friend, he would say. So he kept after me about it, in one way or another, getting me to see the truth about myself, both the good that I was in Jesus and the mess that I was in and of myself, apart from Him. And that watchful gaze of his ultimately changed my life, for through it I came to understand that neither did my sins avert the gaze of Jesus upon my soul. To the contrary, my many shortcomings were exactly what invited God's mercy, and He gave it freely so long as I was truthful and sorry for them. So Doc's ways with me prepared me to meet the gaze of Christ in truth, and this truth, I must say, just as Christ said it would, is what sets any man free.

Let me try to explain this a little more.

Doc's primary work with us was to correct what he called our "false consciences." He believed most people have an incorrect understanding about God and what it is He expects of them. We all believe, correctly enough, that God expects souls to be good. That being so, the question is what happens when souls see that they are sinners, when they begin to realize, as St. Bernadette said of the sinner, that they not only sin, but that they "love sin"? Most of us feel that any such disposition to sin, if really so about us, would separate us from God. And so the usual tactic is to sweep such awareness under the rug, psychologically speaking. And it's true, the relentless mechanisms of repression and self-justification are generally quite effective in hiding our shortcomings from us. Who wants to see the worst about himself or herself? It usually takes some unwanted circumstance to force that knowledge upon us, helped perhaps by the hands of a spiritual director. If so, it's a grace, for when such a director, in one way or another, brings us to face the failed side of our nature, things begin to happen in our spiritual life, things that can be extremely painful at first, things that come under the rubric of self-knowledge. But self-knowledge can lead a soul, reduced thereby like nothing else, to the existential encounter with Christ and his mercy. And with that encounter, lives are changed.

Pope Francis put this all most beautifully:

> We cannot understand this dynamic of encounter which brings forth wonder and adherence if it has not been triggered by mercy. Only someone who has encountered mercy, who has been caressed by the tenderness of mercy, is happy and comfortable with the Lord. . . . I

Liberation

dare to say that the privilege locus of the encounter is the caress of the mercy of Jesus Christ on my sin."

Not everyone, perhaps, but certainly a significant number of those who lived with Doc over the years can be said to have experienced profound, personal change, a change that can best be described as a kind of liberation. It was certainly true that, at the start, living under Doc's tutelage didn't seem very liberating. Just the opposite. In the early days of a relationship with him, most of us needed his watchful eye to correct how we thought, and sometimes even how we behaved. And though the corrections he dished out were essentially spiritual in nature, often as not they would touch on the most ordinary facets of our daily lives, on anything in fact that was convenient to his purpose, like correcting one of the ladies for the way she let her hair droop over her eyes, or one of the guys for the impulsive way he drove a nail.

So, as you might imagine, at the beginning we would be somewhat wary of what he might say to us. But we each of us hung on (it wasn't always easy) because, deep down, we understood that the relationship was healing us and leading to spiritual maturity, both in how we thought and how we acted; and above all else, we believed it was leading us closer to God.

And in the end, the relationship with him would change. For those of us who stayed the course, Doc would begin to treat us as virtual equals, according us the same dignity and freedom that he himself enjoyed, the "freedom of the sons of God," as Scripture puts it. He used to say to me, "Paul, you can get what I have from the same source that I do."

The Man I Called Father

Perhaps one telling sign of my so-called "liberation" will be seen in the story I recount below. It tells of a rather unusual, international, high-tech company that I dared to form together with others from our spiritual family, a company that lasted thirty fascinating years and well beyond the lifetime of Doc. The first years of this firm had him as its Chairman of the Board. That the company's second Chairman was the recently retired publisher of *Time* magazine and one-time corporate president of Time, Inc., may suggest why the adjective "unusual" well fits this enterprise. Why would a tiny, obscure company attract someone of his stature? But the biggest reason for the "unusual" adjective lay in the fact that the company was created by a band of individuals hardly qualified for such an undertaking. No one could have imagined, for instance, that someone like me, with a purely liberal arts orientation, could ever have created an advanced, high-tech company that went on to have international reach. But that's exactly what happened. I call the account of this happening "The Logos Story," after the company's name. I believe you'll find it an interesting tale.

The Logos Story

The following account tells the true story of an unusual business venture undertaken in the spirit of the Psalmist's bold declaration, "Unless the Lord builds the house, those who build it labor in vain"(Ps 127:1). The company lasted thirty improbable years, from 1970 to 2000 and thus no longer exists. But, for reasons I trust will be evident, its story seems well worth telling.

Liberation

I

THIS IS A STORY ABOUT A SMALL, multinational company, the Logos Corporation, that was interiorly dedicated to God at the moment of its conception in 1970. Its history during its thirty-year lifetime had been so unusual, it caused a knowledgeable investment banker to say of it at the time, "Logos is not a business, it's a mystery." As you will see shortly, the many unlikelihoods involved in its formation, its product, and its financial history do indeed seem to defy natural explanation. First and foremost there was the unlikelihood that any commercial enterprise begun by penniless people and with sometimes over a hundred well-paid employees could survive on its own for 30 years without ever once realizing a single dollar in profit, in fact, while incurring annual losses often in excess of several million dollars. Yet this was the case with this little company. This circumstance was not because the business was ill-conceived or had nothing worthwhile to sell or was poorly managed. Rather it was because the product—a computer system that translates between natural languages—was so difficult to build, involved such advanced and problematic technology (in those days), that it took virtually all those years to develop it and then get human translators in multinational companies to even begin to accept it. The picture wasn't all negative of course: the Logos translation system was in fact being used profitably (for its users, at least) by well-known multinational companies in a dozen nations of the world. But while this shows that the company had already given something of demonstrable value to the world, it must also be said that, from a financial perspective, this Logos Corporation should have sunk into oblivion countless times over during its thirty-year existence. So this is a story about a company that had all its life mysteriously contravened the economic laws of gravity, a company as it were that had come to walk on water, by the grace of God and some graced individuals who kept it alive.

The second unlikelihood relating to Logos Corporation concerns the fact that the product this company aimed at developing and bringing to market – a computerized translation system – was considered by the best scientific and technological minds of this country back then (in 1970) to be unbuildable. Let me explain. In the earliest days of the computer, back in the 50's, computer pioneer Alan Turing proposed that these new electronic super-calculators should not only be able to crunch numbers but also be able to do things like play chess and translate languages. Turing was prescient about computers and chess, but the case with language translation turned out to be quite otherwise. To be sure, right after his seminal remarks, numerous attempts were indeed begun worldwide to build just such computer translation systems (known as machine translation systems—MT for short). Government funding flowed freely into university-based research projects for ten years until 1966 when a devastating evaluation by the National Science Foundation (published in a document known as the ALPAC Report) almost overnight brought all these efforts to a halt. This famous report, in assessing the achievements of these projects to date, found them unacceptable and unpromising, and concluded that translation by computer was in all probability not

Liberation

feasible. It appeared that natural language is too complex, too ambiguous, too fuzzy to lend itself to logical, numerical treatment by any method then known to the state of the art. By the late 60's the received wisdom was that MT could not be done and, as a consequence, virtually everyone abandoned the field.

The dust had barely settled on this debacle when Logos Corporation was formed (in 1970), to pick up this task and attempt the impossible. It is said that necessity is the mother of invention and so it was in this case—a unique national need had suddenly arisen just then that made another attempt at MT worth considering on the part of the government. And here was a tiny new company, Logos, claiming it could do what Oxford, MIT, Harvard and IBM and many other powerful organizations around the world had tried and failed to carry off to anyone's satisfaction.

The opportunity had to do with the Vietnamese war and President Nixon's intention late in the war to turn the fighting over to the South Vietnamese and bring our soldiers home. It was called the Vietnamization Policy. This was in the late 60's when the U.S. public had grown restless and unsupportive of the long drawn-out conflict. It seemed like a good idea but there was a major problem—to turn the war over to the South Vietnamese forces meant the U.S. had to supply them with advanced military equipment, equipment that they had to learn to use and maintain. This in turn meant that they either had to acquire a good command of English or be given thousands of military training and maintenance manuals translated into Vietnamese for this purpose. Neither solution seemed realistic. Teaching the South Vietnamese forces English so that it could fight our kind of war would take years. And someone calculated that it would take at least seven years to translate the manuals needed. The problem was so serious that an emergency meeting of the President's Scientific Advisory Council was convened at the White House to see what could be done. One of the participants at that meeting, Evrett Pyatt (later to become Under Secretary of the U.S. Navy), suggested using computers to do the translation. Everyone present knew of the negative ALPAC conclusions regarding prospects for this sort of thing, but Pyatt said he had heard tell of a little company that claimed it had a solution. It was worth looking into at least. And so this is where I came in. The little company was Logos Corporation which I had formed just weeks before in anticipation of this very need. I was contacted and brought to Washington at once to make my case.

In retrospect it seems unlikely that a tiny fledgling company of just a few people, with no track record and no money, barely a month old, should be called upon to address a national conundrum of this importance. The qualification that made Logos unique and that brought us to the government's attention seemed pure happenstance – I happened to be the only person in the United States in 1969 who (1) knew some Vietnamese, (2) knew something about computers, (3) knew something about machine translation, and (4) believed he could do the job. I was the farthest thing from an expert in any of these areas, but the combination was unique and did indeed give me an advantage over companies like IBM when they inevitably tried to muscle in on the opportunity. I went to Washington and made my case to a room full of anxious officials who, for all their skepticism, knew they had little choice but to give me a try, assuming I was real. To test this last qualification, they asked me one question about the system I proposed to build for them – how good will it be? I answered, "Not very good strictly speaking, but good enough to do this job." I was told later that had I said anything else I would not have carried the day. That day is still very vivid in my mind. Our company, only just born, could now take its first breath of life.

Logos Corporation soon received a small contract to demonstrate a prototype capability of English-Vietnamese translation. We were given a long list of English technical terms concerning helicopters and were told that on the day of demonstration our system would be asked to translate into Vietnamese twenty pages from a previously unseen Army helicopter manual employing those terms. We had all of three months to build this prototype. Now all we had to do was pull it off. Given the history of this technology, our own lack of genuine expertise, the short amount of time granted us, the fact that we were virtually starting from scratch, our prospects understandably were not considered good. Evrett Pyatt admitted to us later that government experts had chided him for chasing after "fools' gold."

Had those officials in Washington asked me how I was going to pull this off, I would not have known how to answer. The truth is I didn't know. I just felt I could do it, and somehow my confidence must have come across.

Happily the officials at that Washington meeting never asked. I had some rather vague ideas of an approach, not yet really worked out in my mind, but underneath was this bedrock conviction that any difficulties arising along the way would get solved as we went along. Looking back I see that there really was nothing in my academic or professional background that should have allowed me to feel that way, nothing in terms of my conventional secular preparation. As it turns out there was a reason for such boldness, one I did not become aware of until later, and of which I will speak in a moment.

I am by nature a somewhat retiring person. My academic background was in philosophy and theology. During the Korean war, I enlisted in the Air Force and was trained in several languages by Air Force Intelligence. One of them was Vietnamese. This was before any real hint of our country's future involvement in Viet Nam, and to me there seemed to be absolutely no point in learning Vietnamese, not as far as I was concerned personally, and my study of the language was halfhearted at best. I was always good at languages but they never much interested me, and I positively detested grammar and things like parsing. Nor did I ever exhibit any talent for technology or science. Yet, after my conversion to the Catholic faith, in order to make a living I drifted into the computer field. And it was there that I began to read about the difficulty researchers were having in getting a computer to translate natural languages. Before long, I conceived the idea that, you know, I believe I could really build a machine translation system that actually worked. It was this pure naked conviction alone that

Liberation

brought me to the attention of the government at that moment of crisis.

Well before I ever thought of forming my own company, I had gone to see the government's leading expert on machine translation, a man by the name of Zbigniew Pankowicz, to talk about my interest in the machine translation problem. He was a Polish nobleman who came to the U.S. after having been incarcerated in Buchenwald and Auschwicz during World War II. By this point in my life I was a VP in a small software company, and on my own initiative I had begun to look more seriously into this matter of machine translation. I had dinner with Pankowicz on that first encounter and we talked about the possibilities of a Vietnamese system. I remember at one point leaning over the table and saying to him, with the deepest conviction, "I just want you to understand that I can do this." He must have believed me for he spoke of me later to Evrett Pyatt. The rest is history.

The fact that Logos was small, green and virtually penniless wasn't the main reason we were such an unlikely candidate for this undertaking. What made our selection and subsequent accomplishments most unlikely was the kind of people who made up Logos in those days and who would eventually pull off this achievement. It is here in the people that we get to the heart and soul of this story.

II

By the time this opportunity arose in 1970, I was living as a member of a Catholic lay community on a two hundred acre farm north of New York City. The community had been formed some years earlier by this man we called Doc. As described earlier in this volume, he functioned as a director of souls to any and all who came to him for help and guidance. The community that eventually formed around him operated with the blessing of the diocesan auxiliary bishop and had a common economy, rather like a kibbutz. Its members were drawn from every walk of life: teachers, social workers, former nuns, three frequently visiting priests, a lawyer, a cab driver from Israel (who eventually became a convert, along with his entire family), one or two computer specialists, a farmer, a few medical doctors, some engineers, mechanics, a steady stream of fresh graduates from Catholic colleges, dozens of mothers and scores of kids of all ages – all living under obedience as spiritual sons and daughters of this man functioning as a spiritual father. Except for our Vietnamese linguists, all the early workers at Logos Corporation came from this Catholic kibbutz.

As I have been describing earlier in this volume, I too lived under obedience to my spiritual father, and so it was natural that I would approach him first about this idea of forming a company. I told him of the opportunities I foresaw and of my conviction that I could solve this problem. He seemed genuinely interested, if a little cautious. "To do something like this, you will need Ph.D.'s from Harvard," he said. I said if we need them we'll get them. He looked at me for a while and then said, "Well then, do it." That was all I needed. When Logos was formed shortly thereafter, Doc became its first Chairman of the Board.

It takes money to start a company, and our little

Catholic kibbutz lived from hand to mouth and could never have undertaken something like this. We made a few feeble efforts to raise money on Wall Street, and from some individual private investors, all without success; and then, unexpectedly, we received our funding from the most unlikely source of all – a loan from a nun. This sister was a spiritual child of Doc's who came to be with him from time to time. Like all religious she had taken a vow of poverty, but her circumstance was rather unusual. Her wealthy father had given considerable sums of money to her order under the proviso that should his daughter ever need funds at some point or other, she should be allowed to draw from a special account in her name. For this nun, Logos became such an occasion. The loan was not especially large but it was all she had and enough to get us started. A year later we were able to repay it down to the last penny – the only financier ever to be so favored in the long history of this company.

The company got its precious name from Doc in what always seemed to me to be a favor from heaven. As we were getting ready to form this company, we needed to decide on a name. I asked Doc if he would name it for us and he came up on the spot with some kind of playful acronym. I forget what it was but my instant reaction was to reject it. "No," I said, "we ought to have a serious name, a name that really means something." He looked at me quizzically for a moment and then closed his eyes and sank into what seemed like the deepest contemplation. This went on for many long minutes. When he came to, he said simply, "Call it Logos."

Logos began its life in the bitter cold winter of

1969-1970 in a small, unheated milk house on the community farm. At first there were just two of us, my partner and spiritual brother from the community, Clifford C. and myself. We painted the walls and installed a Teletype machine that enabled us to communicate with a timesharing computer in Stamford, Connecticut. Clif was a gifted mathematician who could take my half-articulated notions and program them into cogent software. Working day and night, we began to program the pieces of this system. Sometimes, late at night, it was so cold in the unheated milk house structure that the ink on the Teletype ribbon would be frozen, and nothing would appear when the machine printed – not until the incessant pounding melted the ink. When that first government contract finally came in, we moved to a larger single-room building in town, installed more modern equipment and added more staff from the members of our community. Among these were several teaching sisters who had left their orders in the post Vatican II chaos, a few students just out of high school or junior college, later augmented by a few college graduates, and finally a handful of mothers from the community, mostly with liberal arts degrees. And we found a gentle Vietnamese scholar by the name of Binh who agreed to join our little enterprise. All of these Clif and I had to train from scratch to use computers, and to work with language in the particular way needed.

Three months later, when the time came for our demonstration, a plane load of some twenty-five government officials, experts, and military types jammed into our little facility, among them a Vietnamese army colonel. There were vocal naysayers among them too, one an expert from Rand Corporation who seemed only too eager to spot all our shortcomings. But the angels were with us. We ran the test text through the system and gave the output to the Vietnamese colonel. Our own Vietnamese linguist poured over the results with him. At one point our linguist Binh put his finger on something and said, "Well, that's not right." The Vietnamese colonel peered closer and then stood up and announced. "No, the machine translated that correctly." That was the turning point. Smiles crept over bureaucratic faces all around and, naysayers notwithstanding, we were on our way. Not long after that, Logos got a seven figure contract to build a real, full blown working translation system capable of translating warehouses full of manuals.

Our little company built that system in a year, completing it on time and within budget. The system was tested by the South Vietnamese in Saigon and was judged capable of producing translations that, with post-editing, were found to be of from "good to excellent" quality. Before long, the U.S. Army, Navy and Air Force began sending us piles of manuals. We enlarged our staff and set up a full-scale production line. We had already translated millions of words into Vietnamese when, one morning, we got a telephone call from the Pentagon telling us to stop everything – the war was about to end.

In official reviews after the Vietnamese war was over, Evrett Pyatt cited our project as having constituted one of the outstanding technology success stories of the entire war effort. Indeed, the Pentagon formally acknowledged that the feasibility of large-scale machine translation had now been demonstrated. Zbigniew Pankowicz, who had been the government's technical administrator of the Vietnamese contract, received the Pentagon's second highest civilian award for his role in this project. Our little band of nuns, students, and mothers had indeed chalked up an outstanding success and we were proud as punch. But the original reason for Logos was over. Now we had to find new reasons for being.

That was in 1973, and somehow we survived and, and in part thanks to Logos' achievements in those early days, so has machine translation as a viable technology. Slowly, painfully, from that point on, Logos, and computerized translation in general, began its long crawl back into respectability and technical viability, not only in the U.S. but around the world. Little by little, commercial companies engaged in international trade began to see the benefit of having their manuals translated by computer; computers allowed the task to be done more quickly, more cheaply, and with greater quality control over terminology usage. But as far as Logos was concerned, there were never enough of these customers, never enough of these forward-looking companies to keep the company afloat; it took a continuous flow of venture capital money to do that, and to allow for the development of additional languages and computer platforms. Thanks to these investors, we were able to develop systems for French, German, Spanish, Portuguese, and Italian. We even developed prototypes systems for Russian, demonstrated to intrigued Soviet officials, and for Farsi, the language of Iran, under

Liberation

contract to the Iranian government, just weeks before the radical Islamic revolution in that country began.

Much of our sales and marketing efforts, obviously, had to be conducted abroad. In the early days of the company, we had an office in Saigon, right across from the Parliament building (until the war ended). Later we had sales and customer support offices and operations in Montreal, Frankfurt, and Salerno. In the US, our headquarters moved to Boston, closer to our sources of venture capital, and we opened a marketing office in the Silicon Valley. Our technology center for most of the company's life was in New Jersey. Had you walked through its modern facilities, you would have heard any number of languages being spoken among the employees, whose number at times exceeded one hundred linguists with advanced degrees and highly trained computer specialists. So from appearances at least, the Company appeared to be thriving.

OK, that's Logos Corporation, more or less, from the outside looking in. Now let me tell you something about this Company from another angle, more from the inside looking out.

III

There is a joke that used to be passed around the Logos Board of Directors whenever the Company's periodic financial difficulties seemed about to bury us: *nothing matters so long as we retain the movie rights to the story.* There's not a little truth in that, for the most extraordinary things happened to this company, particularly in the area of finance. The following is a typical example of what I mean. One day in the late 70's the company was down to its last few dollars and could not make its payroll. At the bleakest point, a loose acquaintance of our financial VP walked in one afternoon to chat, learned of our difficulties, and wrote a check on the spot for 100,000 dollars. That sort of thing has happened time and time again where someone or some group would show up and pull the firm back from the brink. This company had almost expired so many times that, after a while, one became inured.

One of those individuals who came and saved the day was James A. Linen, a man who had been President of Time, Inc. and publisher of *Time* Magazine. When he retired from that vast publishing responsibility he took an interest in little Logos, made some timely investments in the Company, got us the contract with the pre-revolutionary government of Iran for a Farsi (Persian) system, and after Doc died, he became our Chairman of the Board. (This was in the late 70's to mid 80's. We had just completed the Iranian contract when the revolutionary government took control; it took us eight years to get paid for our work, in a courtroom of The Hague). Then for a few years we were actively represented in the marketplace by the famous sports management company, IMG, that was built by Mark McCormick and Arnold Palmer and that still handles many of the premier sports figures of our time. We were even championed for a time by Charles Van Doren and The Encyclopedia Britannica. George Steinbrenner, who was later to become owner of the New York Yankees, played a critical financial role in Logos at one point. (Each of these is an interesting story in its own right.) We had investments by some of the most outstanding investment banks and venture capitalists in the world, including the wealthy French Schlumberger family, one of the Wall Street Lerner brothers, Bessemer (the great granddaddy of American venture capitalists), American Research and Development, Houghton Mifflin, Germany's auto giant BMW, several German insurance companies, and so on.

The list of organizations and financiers who became intrigued with Logos was long indeed. Almost always they first sent skeptical experts to investigate our technology, and invariably the experts' recommendations were positive. A computer scientist from Poland after listening to a detailed explanation of our approach, exclaimed that the system "blew his mind." One analyst from Wall Street, a foreign-born gentleman particularly sensitive to the value of language, said he ranked what we were doing on the first rung of technological achievements of the 20th century. Excessive as these statements must seem, there obviously had to have been something analogous taking place in the minds of investors who continued to pour money into the Company year after year, always without return. Whenever an investor had had enough, and naturally all did after a time, others would always appear to take their place. On average, this infusion of capital has amounted to at least two million dollars per year for 30 years. In the last few years of the company's life, the infusion had been closer to twice that sum.

Clearly these investors all had visions of gold at the end of the rainbow. But the reasons for their investment were more complex than that. The most important backers over the years always said they were attracted to

Logos partly because of its religious background. They felt that the Company and its technology somehow seemed "destined" to make an "important technological contribution to the world" (paraphrasing their own words), and that this feeling made their subsequent losses a bit less troublesome. No one likes to lose money, of course, but losing it for a worthy cause seemed to reduce the bitterness. The Company's last round of investors from Germany were no exception in this regard. This particular group had been following the company for a number of years, and on the occasion of their investment they alluded to the company's religious origins as relevant to their investment decision. They did not try to understand that origin, or probe it, but they were well aware of it, and I was given to understand that they made their investment in part because of it. I mention this because it suggests that the motivations of such men can be more subtle and nuanced than one gives them credit for.

In what way can it be said that this company had a spiritual aspect? Well, looking back at it today, probably nothing would directly suggest such a thing, except for the on-going miracle of its survival. But for the first fifteen years of the company's life, a large picture of Our Lady of Guadalupe hung in the company's main conference room for all to see, investors, prospective customers, visiting experts, whomever. But more tellingly it was the people who worked for this company. Doc once said the real genius of Logos lay in the spirit of cooperation of its workers. And it was true. We were able to accomplish what we did because we worked as if with one mind. There were no serious, disruptive ego problems, no interpersonal undercurrents of criticism, no holding back or dragging of feet, no withholding of information to gain advantage, only willing cooperation with everyone pulling together, doing his or her best to make work whatever it was we were doing at any given point. The common good was everything (after God). As the technological leader, I felt as though I had scores of minds and hands as extensions of my own. And they were good minds and capable hands. There seemed nothing we could not do, could not solve, working in that spirit. In later years, when the original workers from the lay community became a small minority in Logos, the culture of cooperation nevertheless survived, perhaps not without its flaws, but enough to make Logos a rather different kind of company in the estimation of virtually all who knew it or worked for it.

Truly, this way of working must have been pleasing to God, for very quickly in those early days we got into extremely deep waters, technologically speaking, and had to feel our way and make technological decisions on a daily basis that could easily have ruined us down the road if they were wrong. But, strange as this may seem, they rarely ever were. There is something truly remarkable about that fact, given the difficulty of the undertaking, the modest educational level of those doing all this work, and the fact that we really didn't know what we were doing before we had to do it. We worked as one, in the beginnings sometimes as long as 16 hours a day, and always, it seemed, the result in the end had a beautiful rightness about it. A senior project engineer from Apple Computer who had come to work for us, a technical wizard with two advanced degrees, after working with the innards of our system said he'd never in his career seen any technology quite so elegant. Some facets of the system, he said, made him want to "leap out of his chair."

Probably it was an advantage that none of us had ever been formally trained for this work, for it allowed us to do our jobs with completely open minds, minds that could be moved to see and do the right thing. I myself have always felt that the myriad little lights or inspirations that enabled us to solve each problem as it arose, and that in the aggregate went to make up the company's technology, were given to us as gifts. There's no other explanation for it in my mind. I say this with some authority since I was the so-called intellectual father of this system and ought to know. What I know is that, speaking for myself, I was never more than an instrument of the things that we are able to accomplish.

My spiritual formation at the hands of Doc taught me to believe that God has a great deal to do with our daily work, that if we ask him He blesses the work of our hands, and even more, that He does it with us. There is nothing extraordinary in this actually. As St. Thomas taught, it's in the nature of things for God to be the primary cause, and for us to be but secondary causes, of all the good that we do. As Jesus said, "Without Me you can do nothing." It's true that not many people work this way, not consciously, particularly when it comes to technical work. But Doc most certainly did, as did eventually those of us who lived under his direction. He made working in this spirit an intrinsic and necessary part of our formation. Let me elaborate on this a bit.

Liberation

Doc liked to build things, mechanical devices made of Mecanno, and high-fi assembly kits put together transistor by transistor, wire by wire. He even built several harpsicords from kits. Doc had me work with him this way for the first five years that I lived with him, often at night after coming home from my job, on into the early mornings, and especially on weekends. We worked as monks, keeping recollected even as we focused completely on the task at hand. No anxiety about the work was ever allowed to mar the peace of these hours, working sometimes halfway through the night. If a difficulty arose, which it often did, the routine was to quietly review the work up to that point, go over the steps, break the problem down, whatever, always believing that it would turn out right, never allowing the imagination to cloud a relentless objectivity, never allowing anything to destroy the confidence and peace.

Once, I recall, we were making a model gearbox with three forward speeds and one reverse speed. Some problem arose in getting it to shift gears smoothly that seemed to stump us. We were working early in the morning and as it became time for Mass, we put our tools down and went off to church. After communion Doc went into contemplation, as was his custom. This time, when he came out of it, he looked at me and announced that Mary had given him the solution to our gearbox problem. We went straight home and indeed the problem was taken care of. Now, that sort of thing just amazed me at the time, that Our Blessed Mother would take an interest in something so trivial as a model gearbox, and that she even knew anything about gearboxes (though of course that's silly, but I was a recent convert and Mary was new to me).

This is not just a "cute" story, because a real formation was taking place in connection with this work. Doc believed that God is involved in the rightness of everything we do. I lived and worked along side of him for a number of years and came to believe the same thing, that whenever I undertook some piece of work, I was never on my own, never doing it alone. Any task given to me to do, however trivial, held God's interest every bit as much as my own, and could be done with his help, or to put it more accurately, would be done with me as his instrument. My job was to keep myself open and recollected. That was how all of us worked in the early days of Logos, when all the employees were products of this spiritual formation. To be sure, it didn't mean you became passive – we had to apply ourselves to do the work much as anyone, but we believed we were never doing it alone, working out of our own resources. It was not that you necessarily thought about God when you worked or consciously prayed. Generally you couldn't, not if the work was intricate or demanding, which it usually was. But when a difficulty arose, it made all the difference in the world what you did next. You could get quiet and turn to God expecting the answer, or you could become anxious and try to force one by yourself. It made all the difference in the world which.

I don't mean to suggest here that little lights were always popping off in our heads. Sometimes, perhaps, but most of the time it had to do with the way you went about a task. In my own personal experience, whenever a problem arose, my first reaction would be to try to force a solution. It would usually take the direction of increased complication, and it was usually never really satisfactory. When this happened, sometimes a red light would go on in your head, causing you to back off and open your mind to other possibilities. That's when you'd get a little light, an instinct to do it another way. The answers God gave like that were always simple and worked just right. You didn't come to this way of working first off. You generally had to be driven to it by your own mistakes. Mistakes taught you what not to do. In once sense, mistakes were your friend. But after a while, as you learned the right way to work, the mistakes didn't have to be so egregious, although they were always there and always useful. A professor of industrial management science was brought in by an investment group once, to study the way we went about our work. In the end he expressed amazement at the extent to which the company's work was driven by what he called "counter-factual evidence." He said this was unique in his experience. He said the disposition of most people when they work is to see where what they are doing is right. At Logos, he said we had almost a lust to see where it was wrong, so that we could make it better. That way of working came directly from Doc.

Some years before Logos came along, Doc and I, working in this spirit, built an electrically driven power train for a model automobile that comprised a three-speed gear box, an operable clutch and a working, rear-wheel differential that did all the things that real automobiles do when they turned tight corners. It was rather neat, actually, and Doc suggested I take it to my place of work and show it around, which I did. I happened to be employed at that time as a systems analyst for a nonprofit think tank that was designing command and control systems for the Strategic Air Command (SAC). I showed the model around, including to some of the higher-ups. In a way it seemed like a naive thing to do at the time, and I would never have done it on my own initiative. But as it happened, some years later, one of those higher-ups who had been impressed with this model far more than I realized, became the catalyst to a major investment in the early days of Logos, just in time to take over when that first loan by the nun was running out.

I do not mean to suggest that secondary causes do not have a vital role to play in the God-man nexus. I said earlier that I was never particularly interested in languages, but I was good at them and doubtless Logos would never have been formed had this not been the case. Once, as a young man, while I was studying Greek at Hunter College one summer, the professor put a long Greek sentence on the blackboard and proceeded to lecture us about its grammatical properties for twenty minutes. When she was through, she asked if there were any questions. I raised my hand from the last row and said that I was unable to explain why, but I felt that the sentence was ungrammatical. Naturally all eyes turned to look at this odd character in the back of the room, but the professor, bless her, turned to the sentence and studied it. It happened that I was right, and for the rest of the summer this professor (she was chairperson of the Classics department) never ceased thanking me, and encouraging me to study language. There was another incident like that at Logos. We had just finished translating our first military manual, an Air Force instruction

Liberation

book on instrument flying. It had been translated by machine, post-edited by one of our Vietnamese engineers, and finally reviewed by our top linguist, Binh. It was all set to be delivered to the Air Force and I was just browsing through it when something struck my eye. I could not really understand the Vietnamese, but a sentence, rather long, in the middle of this thick manual jumped out at me as ungrammatical. I showed it to Binh and I was right. So there's some kind of curious gift I was born with that allows me to tune into languages at a structural level, a gift that probably has no conceivable utility outside of the use I would eventually put it to. I was flying with a friend once on a Lufthansa flight and had spent the last half hour absorbed in a German newspaper. "What's it say?" my friend wanted to know. "I have no idea," I replied. "I've been reading the syntax."

Although I was subsequently trained in Vietnamese, my original language training in the Air Force was in Russian. For a short time in my Air Force career I used to listen to Russian pilots converse over their radios and would try to glean intelligence from their chatter. It required a solid foundation in Russian to be able to do something like that, and to this end the Air Force conducted an intense Russian language training program that went on six hours a day for 18 months, where the students heard and spoke nothing but Russian. I heard about the program before getting into the Air Force and conceived the notion that this was for me. This was at a time when the Korean War had just started and young American youth were being drafted and sent as green troops into Korea. That prospect didn't particularly appeal and so when my draft notice arrived, I enlisted in the Air Force, hoping against hope that I might get into this language school. I loved Russian literature with a deep passion and the prospect of reading these authors in their own language seemed too good to be true. During Air Force basic training, I found out that there was indeed a slight possibility of getting into that school, but the odds were not especially good. By now I wanted this schooling so badly that I made a deal with God. If he would get me into that school, I promised I would use these language skills for his honor and glory. That prayer was uttered from the heart, for I faced the prospect of spending my four-year enlistment doing something I cared nothing about. But my prayer was heard and soon I received word of my assignment to language school. I thanked God from my heart and worked hard at mastering the language. After completing the Russian program and working for a while listening to these pilots, I received another assignment, this time to study Vietnamese, which I undertook with considerably less passion. But a deal is a deal, and God held me to it (I would not be writing this story today were it not for that pact). At the time this story begins, though, the deal was surely more in his mind than in mine.

IV

Now I must tell you something that occurred to me when I was only four or five years old, when the seed of this technology was planted in my mind, when (as I believe) the finger of God touched my mind in a special

Liberation

way and prepared me for this undertaking later in my life. I do not expect all my readers to accept this, but as far as I am concerned I have no doubts that this is the true beginning of the Logos story as told above. It is this childhood event that accounts for the fact that I could appear before a government board in a moment of crisis and announce, with deepest conviction, that I could solve the seemingly unsolvable problem facing the government, even while not yet knowing quite how I was going to be able to do that. And also for that fact that someone such as I could convince so many financiers through the years that Logos had something very special indeed. This, then, is that inner story.

For a period of perhaps a month, when I was four or five years old, before starting kindergarten, every morning after my father had dressed, eaten breakfast and then disappeared down the cellar stairs to the garage for the trip to his office, I would go straight to my parents' bedroom and look in the wastepaper basket for something I urgently needed. The Pilgrim laundry service that did my father's shirts in those days had the practice of folding up its ironed, starchy white handiwork around a piece of cardboard and of holding it all together with a light blue paper band. Every morning my banker father would take out a fresh shirt, break open the band, and dump it and this all-important piece of cardboard into the wastepaper basket by his bureau. There, unbeknownst to anyone else, I would come on my mission to rescue this critical item the moment the path was clear. This all took place at the height of the depression in 1933 or 1934. I still can see the dark blue and white Pilgrim delivery wagon that once a week delivered my father's freshly laundered white shirts. The wagon had an electric motor and tires of solid rubber and would creep up to our curb without a sound like some huge feline animal. To me the wagon was delivering raw material vital to my first real undertaking in life.

One side of the cardboard was glossy white, and very inviting to the eye of a little boy. I had been collecting these cardboard pieces every day for some weeks until I had a pile of about twenty of them all neatly stacked. Then began an unusual project that in retrospect seems unlikely for a boy that age. I took these cardboards and proceeded to design an abstract system with about 20 interacting components, each cardboard piece representing an important function of the whole. On one cardboard I would draw a graph (an actual two-dimensional matrix of some sort, with a suggestion of plots), on another something that looked like a complex tic-tac-toe construction, with certain boxes blackened and others left white. On other charts I drew what to memory seems like strings of number groupings with boxes drawn around them. On still others I drew networks of lines and circles. Each of these cardboards had a unique, specific function in my mind, but a function that was entirely abstract, unrelated to anything real, anything that I could have articulated.

I still vividly recall sitting against the wall in my parents' bedroom one morning in particular, the sun streaming in on me through the windows, making some new entry on one of the cardboards, perhaps a new number, or a new line somewhere, and then having to adjust two or three other cardboards to reflect this change elsewhere in this system. It was serious work and I would sit this way, morning after morning, shuffling through this stack of cardboards as if I were maintaining a system of real importance. It was a purely formal work in the sense that the system did not relate to anything real, not even in my mind. The system was entirely self-referencing, where each chart seemed to have intricate connections with one or more of the others, but where the system as a whole had nothing to do with anything beyond it in the real world. What held my fascination was simply these interrelationships and interdependencies among the various components, the fact that what happened on one chart had implications for other charts. This activity forms one of the most vivid experiences of my childhood. Everything was done with great deliberation and intensity. I still recall the pleasure and deep satisfaction over what I had done, and this sense that I had discovered something very special, something no one else knew, something terribly important though I could never have explained why it was important or even what it was exactly. I don't recall how it ended. Probably I ran out of ideas as to how to make those components interact. At any rate I soon lost interest in it.

 I never thought again about that childhood adventure until years later during the early days of the Vietnamese project. We were trying to raise some money at a point where the funds from that nun were running out. I had been in contact with one of the higher ups at that think tank I had worked for ten years previously, a person who had been especially impressed by the power train I had shown around the office, the one Doc and I had built together. This individual liked what he heard about

Logos and put together a group of thirty financiers each of whom was asked to throw in $10,000 as a "crap shoot." But first there had to be a technical evaluation. They sent a computer specialist and I proceeded to demonstrate our system. I put in an English sentence and moments later out came the Vietnamese. I could see at once that the translation was wrong. This computer specialist would never have known the difference, of course, and I could have passed it off as perfect. But it isn't in my nature to do that, so I told him it was wrong, but that I knew why and could fix it. I went into a table in the computer memory and changed a single number and then ran the sentence again. This time it came out quite different, and quite correct. The individual was stunned that a single change in a single table could produce such a different effect and he reported back that we had something at Logos that looked very good. Shortly after we got the funds. It was then that I myself realized the connection between the system we were building and that childhood game I used to play, where a single change in one table affected all the other tables in my set of cardboards. In subsequent years I often reflected on this connection – and the feeling I have today about the present Logos system is exactly that feeling I had when I was five, of something special, of something given.

The account of Logos Corporation and its technology that has been given here may seem rather overblown to the reader; but as must be evident by now, I am given to seeing God's hand in everything that happens. And if I have seemed to toot a human horn in this account, it was never my intent. It is God's work I wish to celebrate. The Tower of Babel and the multiplication of languages arose as a consequence of mankind tooting its own horn, of man thinking he could do great things on his own, without God. The Tower of Babel was to reach to the high heavens as a monument to human greatness. God saw it as an act of pride and prevented them from completing it by confusing their language, leading to the so-called Babel of languages that we have today. It's interesting, though, that God was not against the Tower as such, only against their wanting to build it without Him. The 18th Century German mystic, Anne Catherine Emmerich, received a revelation to that very effect:

> "The building of the Tower of Babel was the work of pride. The builders aimed at constructing something according to their own ideas, and thus resisted the guidance of God. . . . They thought not of God, they sought only their own glory. Had it been otherwise, as I was distinctly told, God would have allowed their undertaking to succeed." (From *The Visions of the Venerable Anne Catherine Emmerich, as recorded in the journals of Clemens Brentano.*)

❖ ❖ ❖

Logos Corporation never did succeed as a commercial enterprise. In retrospect, it seems that its reason for existence was never commercial. It provided for the well-being of its employees and gave budding careers to many who needed them. But the fate of its technology may just possible be different. Logos technology was widely recognized as first-class. When the company closed its doors in 2000, German interests acquired rights to the translation system and all its associated technology, and in 2005, a prestigious, quasi-government, German technology institute (DFKI), recognizing its value, undertook to offer the Logos system and associated technology over the Internet to universities and translators free-of-charge, especially to those interested in exploiting the system for third-world languages. This so-called "open-source" system is today called OpenLogos, and several universities in India are currently using components of OpenLogos to develop an English-Hindi machine translation system. DFKI reports that some thousands of translators have downloaded this cost-free OpenLogos system from their website in Germany. A high-tech institute in Portugal is currently looking into the possibility of combining the *linguistically oriented* technology of Logos with the newer *statistical* approaches such as are now available on the Internet. Whether effective hybridization of these two very different translation technologies can be accomplished remains to be seen; but the idea is to combine the unique advantages that each of these methodologies possesses over the other, and thus to produce translations superior to what each can accomplish on its own. So who knows, perhaps it may be that what was begun so long ago may yet have a future, and that only then can the full Logos story be told. I expect it might well be an interesting story, given the hands in which all future things rest.

One last thing remains to be stressed. The company and its world-class technology would never have come

Liberation

into existence were it not for the spiritual effect that this man called Doc had on the company's founder and the chief architect of its technology. And I use the term "chief architect" here in the restricted sense of a secondary causality, for I believe with all my heart and mind that the remarkable technology this company produced was something that was given to it by Our Lord, quite apart from anything we might have concocted on our own. Our chief work was to be open to and make good use of the inspirations given, just in the way this man I called father was wont to do.

In the chapter that follows, I try to tell you about this man in greater depth, about his background, and about what he was up to before he arrived that fateful day at my door in Greenwich Village.

The Man, My Father

O Lord, the depths of a man's conscience lie exposed before your eyes. Could anything remain hidden in me, even though I did not want to confess it to you? In that case I would only be hiding you from myself, not myself from you.
                    —Confessions of St. Augustine

Doc was born in 1903 in New York City of Russian Jewish parents. His father was a successful, hardworking, rather colorless dentist, his mother a domineering woman of considerable intelligence and charm. I do not recall the father's name but I think it was Harold. His mother's name was Eva, a circumstance that caused Doc to quip that he spent much of his life getting "even." Neither of his parents practiced their Jewish faith, although Doc had been duly circumcised and bar-mitzvahed. Doc was nevertheless proud of his Jewishness and when he became a Catholic he never ceased to be a Jew among the *goyim*. Doc viewed us at times with a mixture of amusement and pity, particularly for the way we *goyim* felt obliged to overlay the cruder parts of our nature with refinements of one kind or another. What he saw for the most part was repression, not sublimation. He went to great lengths to free those of us who lived with him from this denial of what goes on beneath the surface, and many over the years took on something of his freedom and spontaneity though never quite his Jewish earthiness.

His parents lived in a large comfortable apartment on Central Park West. They were affluent but not exactly what you would call wealthy. The family was well-connected and moved naturally in the cultured, upper middle class circles of Jewish society in New York.

Doc never had a close relationship with his father, a distant man from all indications, though a faithful provider to his family. By contrast, Doc's mother looms very large in his life and he spent a good part of his life struggling against her and the great ambitions she had for her precocious firstborn. Doc had been a phenomenally gifted child, displaying the sort of intellectual precocity so cultivated and celebrated in New York Jewish circles. He also gave signs at a very early age of a most unusual gift for the piano. It was not long before his mother recognized her son's gift and turned him into a serious piano student with long mandatory hours at the keyboard every day. The gift for music was his but the ambition was hers entirely. His recollection of the piano in those years was that of always trying to play faster than his hands and musculature would allow, so much so that much of his youth he said was filled with frustration. Worse in his eyes was his mother's wont to show off his playing before streams of friends and visitors. Doc's musical endowments were indeed quite extraordinary but under the circumstances he developed very complicated feelings about the piano and as a teenager almost broke down over it. When Doc became a Catholic at the age of thirty and ultimately sought a life of obscurity in the service of God, his mother's disappointment in her firstborn was boundless. *What a waste,* she would say. *He has such a gift. Now who will know it?* It meant nothing to her when Doc would say he could only play the piano for God's honor and glory; she wanted what she felt was her rightful portion. It would not be an exaggeration to say that Doc struggled to get out from under the shadow of this woman for much of his life. It was revealing to see how this grown man could still be unsettled by his mother even in her old age. But for all the turmoil, there was always a great bond between them and when she grew ancient and feeble she came to live with him. And just before she died, she too became a Catholic.

When a career in music seemed out of the question, Doc decided he would become a medical doctor and went off to the University of Michigan as a pre-med student. He proved to be a brilliant undergraduate student both in humanities and the sciences and got into medical school with no difficulty. But in medical school he discovered a second failure: he could not cope with the rote memorization called for in anatomy courses. He explained he could not learn something without knowing the reasons for it's being the way it was. Anatomy wasn't taught that way and after a painful first year he dropped out and returned home, leaving his brother behind to carry on the family's medical tradition.

Doc then went to Paris for a time and circulated in the artist community there. The artists welcomed him for his keen mind and no doubt for his skills at the piano, but though he immersed himself in the bohemian scene, he found he could not take it too seriously. He told the story of one exchange between himself and a Left Bank artist friend who had asked him to view his latest work. *What do you think?* the artist asked Doc, showing him a large abstraction. Doc studied it for a while and said whimsically, *I see mice climbing a ladder. Oh, no!* the artist cried, horrified. *Space, just space!*

Doc wound up going to Columbia University for a doctorate in philosophy. He took a course in Ethics given by Richard McKeon and, ever the wit, caused it to be known as a class in Dickey McKeon Ethics (playing on Aristotle's *Nicomachean Ethics*). Doc turned out to be a brilliant student with a great fondness for Aristotle, and he soon became known for making outspoken Aristotelian-like observations during classes in modern philosophy. This practice became so unsettling to one of his professors that the distraught man, at wit's end, appointed Doc the class's official Aristotelian commentator.

Doc was Aristotelian by nature and his attraction to this Greek philosopher naturally lead him to explore St. Thomas' commentaries on Aristotle. This encounter changed his life forever. Up to this point in his life, Doc had been an agnostic, but the encounter with St. Thomas and this saint's faith made a deep and permanent impression. Doc began to read this medieval theologian in earnest, and before he was through he believed in God the way St. Thomas believed, which is to say with his whole mind and heart.

He wrote his dissertation on the philosophy of music. It was not to be a study of other men's thoughts on this subject but an entirely original theory about music and the basis for its effects on the emotions. The paper had few footnotes and little bibliography. Doc said that he typed the first and only draft of his dissertation directly onto stencils. The submission was approved by the review committee without revision, enabling him to receive his doctorate two years from the date he began his studies. With that credential in hand Doc set off on an academic career.

His first appointment was to Chicago University where he taught in the Great Books program under Ralph Hutchins. He also taught courses in music theory and appreciation. It was during this period that he was received into the Church. And from this point on his immersion in the Catholic faith became total; he became a daily communicant and devoted himself wholly, mind and heart, to the understanding and love of God. He was instrumental in bringing many others into the Church during this period, especially Jews, so much so that the Jewish Rabbi's associated with the University began to complain. He became good friends with Mortimer Adler, a fellow Jew and faculty member who came to share some of Doc's appreciation for St. Thomas but who drew the line at conversion, although I have heard that in his later years, Adler too embraced the faith. Doc told a funny story about the latter scholar. The two of them had been invited to a Catholic convent for dinner one evening by a sister who was studying at the University. One of the nuns, serving Adler a plate of soup, teasingly remarked that the soup had been made with holy water. Adler is said to have sat up in his chair exclaiming, *What does it do? What does it do?* Adler and Doc later had a falling out when Adler published an essay attempting to refute the Thomistic arguments for the existence of God, and in rebuttal, Doc published a decimating refutation of Adler's reasoning. They were never friendly after that, though Doc must have gained stature in Adler's mind. Some years later, Adler told a mutual acquaintance, who related it to me, that in his estimation "Doc was the greatest logician the West has had in the last 500 years. This was typical hyperbole for Adler, but Doc produced that impression on many academics.

Doc next received an appointment to St. John's College in Annapolis, where a similar Great Books program was underway under Scott Buchanan. Here it seems Doc came into his own as a luminary figure on campus and came to be regarded as an intellectual giant of sorts. I was in Washington DC on business in the late '60s and happened to meet a young man who had just graduated from St. John's. It had been nearly 30 years since Doc taught at St. John's and I wondered if Doc was still remembered, so I asked the young man if he had ever heard of him. *Are you kidding?* he said, looking at me as if the question couldn't be serious.

Doc was not happy with his role at a secular university. He wanted to teach in a Catholic institution and to serve God by bringing young minds to a love of God as his had been brought. By this time he had become something of an authority on the philosophy and theology of St. Thomas, which ought to have qualified him to teach in a Catholic university, but his secular credentials did not make him attractive to philosophy and theology departments still comprised mostly of priests in those days. His being a Jewish convert did not exactly help either. But Doc persisted. He got a temporary appointment at the Jesuit Georgetown University, during which time he also came into fateful contact with the neighboring Dominicans at the Dominican House of Studies of the Province of St. Joseph (encompassing the northeastern USA). It was during this period that Doc conceived his life-long love for the Dominican Order of Preachers.

While at Georgetown, he turned his own house on Otis Street into a center for lively, free-wheeling discussions about the faith and the life of faith. Priests, particularly the Dominicans, and students alike flocked there and before long he was surrounded by disciples and admirers all drawn irresistibly to his brilliance and personality. But far more than that, they were drawn by something which was to become his hallmark – his uncanny grasp of how to make God practical in one's life. He had this uncanny ability to make the far reaches of Catholic mysticism – of intimacy with God – seem accessible to the confused and often anxious souls who came to him, both clerical and laity. Lives were changed, spiritual lives were deepened, and vocations sprang up, perhaps not in great number but in great depth of quality. I can say this because years later I got to know some of these remarkable people who came under Doc's influence at this time, people who would have a great effect on my own life.

Before long Doc became a regular visitor to the Dominican House of Studies and his influence there among the young seminarians and certain of the faculty spread like a blaze in dry summer grass. There was indeed something about his mind and powers of articulation that was irresistible, that simply mesmerized his listeners, especially when the talk turned to spiritual matters. He could answer virtually any question you asked, not with a quick bright answer shot from the hip, but with something usually mind-blowing that came from you-knew-not- where. Often as not, his first response to your question was to ask you a question – nothing pleased him more than a good, well-formulated question. Often, the question you wound up with was quite different from the one you started with, and more telling. Once he felt he had the question you were really asking, he would close his eyes and go into deep reverie, maybe for minutes. Was he praying, or thinking, or listening? We never knew exactly. Then he would open his eyes and begin to talk. What he said would send all kinds of electric currents through you and make you lean forward in your chair. If you were the one to ask the question, the reply was invariably tailored to fit your case, your capacity, your perhaps only half-articulated difficulty. Not only that but he could take the driest, most obscure theological issue and show how it mattered to your life. In private conversation he would show you how your emotional problems actually had their genesis in a misunderstanding of your relationship to God, in what he called a *false conscience*, and he would persuade you that true mental health was fully possible only in the practice of the true faith. And he did all this by making you laugh and feel good and hopeful about yourself, even when what he said might hurt a little. *If the shoe fits don't throw it at me*, he used to tease, erasing your frown with pursed lips and a knowing look. He could talk with this uncanny authority of his about virtually anything – about theology, Scripture, philosophy, psychiatry, physics, mathematics, art, music, literature, virtually anything – but above all and most important, about what made a person tick. He seemed to know what made *you* tick. After a while you hung on every word, and missed thoughts of his would get passed around like precious jewels. I was not there at the House of Studies but I was party for many years to similar experiences much later on, so I know first hand what I am talking about.

The experience had nothing to do with the sort of mental sparring that goes on in universities, where every so often some professor will be so utterly brilliant and often so arrogant that others enjoy playing foil, just to see how he will manage to have the last word. This experience was nothing like that. Nor had it anything to do with pontification. It was more like sitting in front of someone plugged into God's Truth. He was indeed like the ultimate answer man, where the questions were the deep often personal ones that no one had ever found answers for and sometimes didn't even know how to ask. And his answers had the ring of truth; the more you shook them the truer they rang. Once you experienced this, you found you couldn't get enough of it. Add to that his keen Jewish wit and, worse in some eyes, his indomitable personality and you can imagine the effect he had on those around him.

Doc cultivated this contact with the Dominican seminarians and priest faculty members with all the energy at his command, but apart from a small number of individual priests who remained close to him all his life, he was eventually shunned by an Order that (as I was led to believe) did not wish to learn its theology from an authoritative layman, and probably least of all a converted Jew. But Doc would never cease to be a Dominican at heart, and though the Order would thereafter keep him at a distance, Doc continued to function as a spiritual father to a small but devoted following of Dominican priests and (former) women religious until the day he died. And, virtually all the lay people who lived in community with him in later years became Third Order Dominicans (T.O.P), including the present writer.

For whatever reason (probably because of their ancient differences with Dominicans on the theology of grace and free will), the Jesuits at Georgetown did not renew his academic appointment, and his life entered a dark and painful period of vocational uncertainty, partially relieved by a temporary teaching appointment at Lavalle University in Montreal. At Lavalle, again he found his real calling in working with priests. To my knowledge, it was here that Doc first broached with priests his views on human sexuality, and, in particular, on sexual repression and its deleterious effect on spiritual maturity. One priest who was present at these discussions later told me that some of his peers found Doc's views difficult to accept.

The difficulty many people have had with Doc on this question is real, far deeper than the mere incompatibility of Jansenist-like attitudes then prevalent in U.S. Catholicism with those of an uninhibited Jew, though that is surely part of the reason for the difficulty. Let it be said here merely that Doc understood the human psyche, and himself, all too well to believe that outright sexual repression could ever contribute to sanctity. Sublimation yes, but not repression. Sexuality is too fundamental to our nature for us to think we can or even ought to go to God without our sexuality being acknowledged and properly dealt with. To him, sanctity presupposed mental health, and as he understood the matter, you do not become healthy by repressing half your nature. For him, the road to both mental health and holiness was to acknowledge these drives so that God can deal with them, however unsavory they might sometimes be (given our fallen nature). He was fond of relating the story about St. Jerome, who in the pursuit of purity would throw himself headlong into briar patches in an effort to beat down an unruly nature. One day, the story goes, Jesus complained to Jerome that he had not given Him everything as he had promised. *Lord,* Jerome replied, *what it is you want? I have truly sought to give you everything. Everything I own, everything I am, body and soul is yours.* Jesus answered, *Yes, Jerome, you have given me all those things but there is one thing you are still holding back: you have not given me your sins.* For Doc, repressed people go to God as half-persons. Indeed, he saw sexual repression as a kind of sickness that militated against sanctity. As you can see, in addition to everything else, Doc was a thorough student of Sigmund Freud. He did not agree with Freud on many things, but as to the reality and force of sexuality there wasn't much argument.

Perhaps Doc's views about this can best be seen in a limerick he composed around this time:

> *I think we're so refined*
> *We drive poor God out of His mind.*
> *I think he was so annoyed,*
> *He raised up Sigmund Freud*

As a Catholic, of course, Doc would never agree with Freud that the sexual drive was primary. That primacy Doc gave to the appetite for God, and for union with Him. What Doc saw was that these two appetites were not unconnected. Indeed, he spent a good part of his life trying to understand and deal with that connection, foremost it seems in himself. The conclusions he came to are compelling. He came to believe that, *given our fallen nature (to the extent that it remains unrectified),* one of these appetites will almost inevitably occasion the repression of the other. It didn't matter especially which one, for either condition was unhealthy, though certainly not equal in God's eyes. On the one hand, the so-called "pious" individual represses (i.e., cannot acknowledge) his appetite for sexual expression, unconsciously doing so in order to avoid feelings of guilt. On the other, the libertine represses his appetite for God, and for the same reason, for if he acknowledged God, his illicit behavior would engender guilt. In both cases repression is virtually inevitable because of the disorders that are latent if not actual in our sexual nature; repression is one way – the wrong way – of dealing with the guilt that such disorder invariably gives rise to. To repeat, in the pious individual, acknowledgement of sexual desires is repressed in order to avoid these guilt feelings, just as in the libertine, acknowledgement of the natural desire for God is repressed, and for the same reason, to avoid feeling guilty. In a healthy, rectified nature, both appetites are freely acknowledged and sublimated to each other in each of their spheres, and provided that the associated activities are ordered as God ordained they be ordered, they form the basis for sanctity. That is to say, the need for spiritual union with God on the one hand, and on the other for intimacy with another creature, should not be experienced as separate, unrelated, and least of all, as warring needs, but rather as integral aspects of a whole person. Sexual expression can be and sometimes is ordained to be wholly sublimated – as in the case of religious – so that all its energies serve to increase the impulse to intimacy and union with God, but repression (i.e., lack of acknowledgement) of sexual energies is only damaging. As St. Thomas taught, grace works through nature. As Doc saw it, when some aspect of that nature is repressed because of latent or actual disorders, nature is crippled and grace is impeded. It was a large part of his mission to try to heal that nature by dealing with repression, by removing misgivings about God and sexuality that had no foundation in truth, even where, in our helplessness, such disorders may operate, nay, especially where they operate. He would teach that sins born of weakness do not separate us from God, as the pious secretly fear, but indeed can be the very stepping stones that God permits in order to bring us to Him, so that, in coming to Him, He might free us of our weakness and transform us. It was Doc's view that Satan, the accuser, has worked the whole world into a corner, indeed, has succeeded in cutting an immense part of human nature off from God because of our false conscience about these matters, with the awful consequence for our times of an unhealthy proliferating libertinism advancing against an often effete, retreating spirituality. He believed it was his calling to oppose that false conscience with enlightened doctrine grounded both in the mystical tradition of the Church and in psychological realism – in short, grounded in truth, in mercy and in the transforming power of God.

Doc's views on the matter of human sexuality were easily misunderstood, almost as if he were condoning free sexual expression. But all he wanted was for people to squarely face their sexuality, to bring it to God and let Him deal with them as they really and truly are.

While he was at Chicago University, Doc got married. His bride, Charleen, had been a brilliant graduate student of his, taking her doctorate in clinical psychology. Her dissertation, which Doc helped her with and indeed largely formulated, dealt with Freud and Scholasticism and was later published as a book under that title. The early years of their marriage were apparently idyllic, she being the perfect, conforming wife, he being the loving and wise head of the home who revered the lady of his life. Doc was proud of Charleen and praised her with great ardor in a series of love poems some of which appear in the next chapter.

At some point after their marriage, but before children were to appear, Doc became convinced that he belonged in a monastery. It seemed that his wife, Charleen, felt the same for herself, and so the two arranged to pursue a religious vocation, he to a monastery and she to a convent. The venture lasted all of one day, for it took Charleen only one night in the convent to realize she did not belong there. As a consequence, Doc was obliged by his superiors to abandon this vocation for himself as well.

Doc finally got a permanent appointment in the philosophy department at Xavier University in Cincinnati, where he taught for a number of years. He was immensely popular there as a teacher but got on less well with the school's Jesuit administration, a circumstance which by now had become a familiar pattern in his life. Eventually, officials in the administration did things that seemed designed to discourage him, such as assigning him back-to-back classes in widely separate parts of the campus, or so he felt at least.

Doc and Charleen bought a big house, adopted two children and then had two more of their own. Gradually, however, the relationship between husband and wife began to change. Charleen opened a clinical practice and developed a following in her own right, a circumstance that took her away from her duties as mother and housewife, duties which Doc found himself filling more and more. The growing independence of his wife and the subtle signals he was getting from the administration led him to once again re-examine his calling. He spent much time in prayer and in shared reflection with his wife about what God wanted of him and of them both. Doc came back to the conclusion that he belonged in a monastery, a decision to which Charleen now gave her full consent. He contacted a Trappist monastery in Colorado and made arrangements to spend time there as a long-term guest. It would be a time for reflection and for testing his vocation. So at the end of the school year Doc left Cincinnati never to return to his family or to teaching again.

Doc's stay at the Trappist monastery proved to be yet another turning point in his life. As always, he became popular with the younger monks, many of whom began coming to him for counseling. Observing his unusual gifts, the abbot felt that Doc indeed appeared to have a religious vocation of sorts, but one that ought to keep him in the world where he could help people more widely, not secluded in a monastery. One suspects that the abbot's reasoning may have been biased by this dynamic presence disturbing the normal order of his monastery. In any case, the abbot sent Doc off with a letter of introduction to his friend, the archbishop of Mexico City. Doc hit it off well with the archbishop, a holy man, and the archbishop did the unprecedented thing of assigning this New York Jewish convert the duties of spiritual director to several contemplative communities, among them a Carmelite convent. In addition, he was asked to teach a class of priests. It is during this period that Doc's spiritual life appeared to come into full flower. He lived like a penurious monk, gave himself to God's work from early morning till late at night and moved among the Mexican people as naturally as if they were his own, despite the paucity of his Spanish. He loved Mexico and the Mexicans and he quickly developed a deep and lasting devotion to Our Lady of Guadalupe. In return, he was loved by all, from the hierarchy down to the simplest Indian peasant. He came to know some very holy women, among them followers and disciples of Conchita Armida, one of whom was the superior of a religious order and a mystic whose cause is now being pursued in Rome. Another was a Mexican woman mystic known simply as Lupita. Jesus revealed himself as a little child to this Indian peasant, a phenomenon which subsequently gave rise to a devotion to the Holy Infant of Good Health (a statue of which Doc brought to Padre

Pio, as recounted in an earlier chapter), and to the erection of a large basilica in Morelia, Mexico dedicated to Jesus as the Holy Infant of Good Health. Lupita loved Doc very much and it is said she spoke to Jesus about him. She related that Jesus told her Doc would be responsible for conversions as numerous as the sands of the sea.

It was the Carmelite convent in particular that embraced Doc as a wise director and ultimately as a greatly beloved spiritual father. He told some of us of the first time he visited this convent. All the sisters were assembled behind their screened-off area for his talk. In broken, halting Spanish, he related to them the story of the woman taken in adultery and about to be stoned for her sins, and then asked the sisters who they identified with in the story: with Jesus, with the Pharisees, or with the adulterous woman. One of the less shy sisters ventured that she identified with the woman, whereupon Doc peered at her and asked, in typical fashion: *And in just what way are you like a prostitute, sister?*

If I seem to suggest in the foregoing that Doc was preoccupied with human failings, that is hardly the case. He wanted us to believe, more than anything, that when we turned away from ourselves to go to Jesus, we were holy and pleasing to God. Perhaps the most pivotal moment in my experience with him had to do with this. One morning, seemingly apropos of nothing, he informed a few of us he had something important to tell us. As we gathered around him, he began to teach us about the Name of Jesus, and at a certain point he looked straight at me and said, "The Name of Jesus is as oil poured forth." I recall feeling a sudden warmth flood my interior upon hearing those words; and the reality of this remark has stayed with me to this day, some fifty years later. Many of us who lived with Doc began to say the Name of Jesus interiorly throughout the day, almost as if with our breathing. Time and time again, when things were difficult, he would remind us to "go the Jesus," and by then we knew that the best and most immediate way to do that was by the prayerful uttering of his Name. We came to believe in the very marrow of our bones that Jesus is most especially attentive to our cries at such times. Not that acknowledgement of sin and the cry for mercy is the only way to go to God, but it is the way for sinners.

Doc knew himself to be a sinner. Most people who knew him took him as someone singularly close to God, which I believe was true. But I once heard him tell a very proper, elderly lady that if she knew the truth about him, about what he was like in and of himself, apart from Jesus Christ, she would drop dead.

The deep, personal, often hidden truths of our unworthiness are not easy to face, as I have been acknowledging throughout this account. Indeed, the need to feel good about ourselves is so deep and pervasive that it is exceedingly difficult if not virtually impossible on our own to face up to evidence to the contrary, at least until one has been blessed with the rectification of self-knowledge. And, invariably, it's a momentous grace when we are able to do just that, for it is precisely in such moments that we come to know God's mercy is for real. Jesus said that He is the *way*, the *truth* and the *life*. Many of us came to know this existentially, that the *way* to new *life* in Christ is precisely through *truth* – deep, personal truth wrapped in the divine mercy of his Cross.

And when souls discover that this mercy is *for them*, as is what happened for many under Doc's tutelage, then these hard, personal truths work to set us free, just as Jesus said the truth would do. And then, indeed, one begins to live a new life.

In these pages I have been describing this man we called Doc, the man I called my father. Obviously, I think he was a chosen soul and singular instrument of God, certainly for my life and that of my family. But this man has had his detractors as well, and some recognition of that fact seems appropriate before I close this account. It is true, Doc still smarts in the memory of certain people who knew him. If one did *not* believe God was behind him, then certainly his manner and methods of dealing with souls could readily be misunderstood and criticized. Regarding detractors, I am reminded of what Jesus said of those who were prepared to stone the woman taken in adultery, "Let him who is without sin cast the first stone." That certainly is wise counsel. In any case, the present author is one who knows he owes his life, spiritually and otherwise, to the ministrations of this unusually gifted man. And he can say, quite simply, that he will be eternally grateful for having been given this man as his father in God.

Made in the USA
Lexington, KY
05 May 2017